The famous Oscar Nemon statue of Sir Winston Churchill stands in a prominent position looking out towards the Dover Patrol Memorial on the white cliffs in the distance. Sir Winston Churchill's grandson, Winston Churchill MP, unveiled the bronze statue on November 30, 1972

I thought I was going to be God's gift to physical training

"I had to recover the bodies of 32 young men - soldiers who had just finished training and were due to go home"

Words by Terry Morgan

Former leader of Bury Metropolitan Council, Mr Albert Little, clearly remembers his time as a physical training instructor (PTI) for the Royal Navy during the war, although he is keen to stress that: "My naval career was quite an experience, but it was certainly not what I would call distinguished, particularly in comparison to the sacrifices other sailors and soldiers made for the war."

Mr Little, who recently turned 89, joined the Navy in December 1939 soon after the Salford primary school at which he had been teaching was evacuated.

Having previously spent time at a physical training college in Denmark, Mr Little said: "I thought I was going to be God's gift to physical training. The scales fell from my eyes when I realised what the standards were in the Navy, as I had no experience whatsoever in trapeze and vaulting."

Mr Little, who now lives in Summerseat, was a PTI Petty Officer from 1940 to 1946.

"My active service however was spent entirely on what were known in the Navy as 'stone frigates' - land-based barracks. I was never posted out at sea; my role was to train the recruits and get them physically fit for service."

For the first few months, Mr Little was at Temeraire, the naval school of physical training, after which he was drafted to Drake barracks in Portsmouth in 1940, during the fall of France.

Soon after, he was transferred to Raleigh in Torpoint near Plymouth - the Navy's principal training facility.

Mr Little jokingly refers to this as his 'sea time.' "I was on the Torpoint Ferry crossing over to Plymouth!"

His 'foreign service' came next, when he was posted to Scotland - first to Scotia in Aire then to Stopford in Bo'ness near West Lothian in 1944.

Although he was not involved in direct fighting, Plymouth was blitzed extensively in 1941 due to its strategic importance as a major naval dockyard, causing widespread devastation.

It was left to the officers and men of the Raleigh to clear and recover the dead in the aftermath. "During one night, I had to recover

Albert Little today

the bodies of 32 young men - soldiers who had just finished training and were due to go home the next day," is one of Mr Little's sadder recollections. Evidently, none that were involved in the war, no matter how remotely, were left untouched by it. Mr Hill was de-mobbed in early 1946 and immediately returned to teaching.

He was appointed headteacher of St Mark's School in Bury and later became headteacher at a school in Middleton.

In 1966, he was elected to the Ramsbottom Urban District Council and became chairman in 1971 - a post he remembers with great fondness - before being made leader of the council for Bury in 1974.

Mr Little does not reminisce too much about the war. When he does, he stoically sees it as something that happened a long time ago - an important event to which he contributed what he could.

"Life goes on," he said. "It always does."

Off on our great adventure...

"There must have been hundreds of boats all around us - a truly remarkable sight"

Words by Terry Morgan

Able Seaman George Stott of Dumers Lane, Radcliffe, was only aged 22 when thousands of men poured from hundreds of ships onto the beaches at Normandy on D-Day.

He recalls: "On Sunday, June 5, we moved anchorage to a position just outside Portsmouth Boom. As we moved slowly between the many troop carriers, we heard the songs of the invading Army - here were the Yanks, the Tommies, the Cannucks and every other nationality all as one, but singing their own particular national songs.

'As it neared midnight, silence reigned except for the lapping of the waves against the mighty ship's sides. Up came the anchor and we were off on our great adventure.

'We had a few hours' sleep and just before dawn, we were piped out of our hammocks and we quickly dressed into warm clothing and waited for the big moment. It was a terribly rough sea and the thought of being lowered into that black swelling turmoil made my stomach turn double somersaults.

'Streaks of dawn on the horizon were the prelude to the anchor dripping noisily into the black inferno. Up went the battle ensign, troops filed into their boats and I found myself stood on the stern of my landing craft waiting to unhook the shackles which would send us on our way.

'Then, the orders came - the booming voice of the skipper, the piping voice of the First Lieutenant - 'Stand by in the boats,' then a prolonged pause............. 'Lower away.'

'We dropped steadily - the waves lashed out bottom and strove to tear us away from our hooks - then came the final order: 'Let go,' and amid the cheers of the ship's company, we buffeted out way, Normandy bound.

'Our escort picked us up and we followed her slowly. There must have been hundreds of boats all around us, landing devices one could never have dreamed of - a truly remarkable sight.

'Planes roared overhead, giving us a feeling of confidence. I was in the leading boat in our flotilla and as I looked back at the other five, directly behind them I saw (in the next boat) the Canadian Padre, his head in his hands praying for the safety of his men. I found myself praying too and I felt much better.

'We crept slowly towards the French coastline and it wasn't long before we could pick out individual landmarks, including two conspicuous church steeples, one of which was our own particular landmark.

'The atmosphere was tense now. I must admit I

George Stott back in his seafaring days and, below, today

was more scared now than ever before in my whole life. Then the sparks started to fly. It seemed as if Krupps armament factory was being thrown at us - mortars, machine gun bullets and rifle fire met us at every angle. Just before we touched down, we encountered long staves with beach mines and barbed wire fastened to them. Our coxswain neatly and skilfully dodged them.

'As we touched the sandy beach, the ramp crashed down. At first, for maybe three seconds, no one moved. Then with a rush, away went the troops, right into the fray. It didn't take us long to get the boat off, but as we moved, we had a miraculous escape as a mortar

fell within a few feet off our port bow. We all felt the blast and experienced the sickly smell of burnt power in our nostrils.

'We steamed full speed for about 15 minutes and then scanned the beach behind us for our other boats. We could still see two on the beach and slowly, one of them came astern but she seemed to be floundering badly as we went to her assistance and tied up alongside her. She was sinking, but we seized buckets and pumps and tried unsuccessfully to bale the water out. It was at this point that I saw my shoes disappear on the tip of a green wave. My socks were inside them.

'At last, we decided to sink her so that there was no chance of her falling into enemy hands, so we opened all the hatches and hopped aboard smartly. We made our way back to our carrier ship which lay four miles out to sea. It seemed as if our chances of getting back were very slim. Our flat bows shook with rage at the cruel waves. We crashed and buffeted, nose-dived, tossed and turned. We didn't seem to move an inch.

'For hours we strived until at last we sighted our goal on the horizon - but that didn't mean our troubles were over. We saw small boats sink like stones in the heavy swell. We saw a destroyer blow up in smoke after being hit by a shore battery and on top of all that, we had a boat full of water. I baled it out with a fellow Seaman. We had two pumps taking it in turns and we never stopped until we reached out ship.

'Even then, our troubles were still not over. We tried time and time again to get alongside our ship, but each time the wind forces us away. I could have cried but I was too cold to even do that. I looked a pathetic figure stood in my bare feet on the stern. At last we made it and we were hoisted carefully back into position on the davits. Was I glad to get aboard a steady and firm ship again!

'We were given an extra tot of rum by the skipper, a good dinner by the ship's chief cook and a well-earned sleep. We had lost two boats out of six. We had brought back the whole crew from one but the other had lost its officer and a rating was badly wounded. He was the best officer we had and he was mourned by all who knew him. The trip back to England was uneventful. We had aboard some army casualties, one a Marine Commando shot through the head. He was buried at sea. We made 17 further trips back to France. We also did mail trips and on one of these, we took Eric Barker and his merry-go-round show. He gave us a bumper show on the deck on the way across."

He cheered us in our darkest hours

A report from the Bury Times dated April 4, 1945

Words by Terry Morgan

Lieutenant Turner

Hero of the gallant but unsuccessful airborne operation at Arnhem last September, Lieutenant Desmond Turner of School Brown, Bury, is back home again on short leave after taking part in landing behind the Rhine.

He described the operation as a tremendous success, summarising it in the phrase "a great show."

The Bury Grammar School old boy and son of Major and Mrs N S Turner, Lieutenant Turner volunteered for the Airborne Division about 18 months ago after serving in the Ack Ack.

The part he played in the Arnhem adventure, when after nine days of bitter fighting the effort to turn the flank of the German armies defending the Reich had to be called off, earned him tributes from his colleagues.

"He cheered us in our darkest hours," said Staff Sergeant Symonds of Manchester, "and kept us going when we were nearly finished."

That landing was a gallant failure, but the Rhine venture was in every way a success.

At Arnhem, the tanks were unable to get to the paratroops in the expected time, but in the Rhine affair contact was established after a few hours.

"The organisation was terrific," said Lieutenant Turner, "and the whole show went without a hitch throughout."

There was, however, one unexpected problem for the Glider Pilots.

"Montgomery boasted they put up the best-ever smoke screen before the crossing of the Rhine was attempted, and it was indeed a most effective screen. So effective that it was only with difficulty that we were able to discern our landing points. At last, we were able to pin-point our position from the white concrete surface of the autobahn."

The excitement began before the gliders touched down, for they came in through the flak thrown up by the German anti-aircraft gunners.

A number of aircraft were lost, but this was inevitable. The paratroops were at once, engaged by the German ground forces, and although some groups were cut off, it was not long before they were relieved.

Then came the tanks and the success of the venture was complete.

Lieutenant Turner spent some days in the Reich and was interested in the reaction of the German farm people to the coming of the Allied armies.

He said: "They were only too eager to do what they could for us and it would appear that the Nazi fanatics have left the farming people much to themselves, so long as they tilled the land and produced the food needed to feed the workers and the soldiers."

Now, Lieutenant Turner is looking forward eagerly to his next 'drop.'

He avers that the life of a Paratrooper is a thrilling and compelling experience.

He declared: "The men are all volunteers and a grand lot they are. This modern arm of warfare will continue to play a big part in the operations leading to the complete military defeat of the enemy."

Jack Lomax with his comrades

The futility of war

"We received a signal to search for survivors. Sadly, we found none"

Words by Terry Morgan

Jack Lomax, from Stand Lane in Radcliffe, was Signalman with the Royal Navy on board Grey Shark. Days before the Normandy Landings, Jack's ship ran the gauntlet along the coast of France while senior officers mapped the locations of the enemy guns which were firing on them.

He recalls: "My recollections start a little before D-Day when our flotilla of four ships came under American command. We worked with them in their exercises, including the disaster at Lyme Bay, Dorset, where they practised landings on Slapton Sands.

'We were patrolling another sector when apparently German E Boats - fast torpedo crafts - got among the exercise and sunk two large landing craft and damaged a third. We received a signal to search for survivors. Sadly, we found none. Some 750 Americans died that night.

'A few nights before D-Day, our ship was given a special mission to collect an officer and his colleague who came on board with lots of charts and we set course for Cherbourg. I was Signalman and heard and saw what took place.

'We stopped in the darkness just off the Mole and the skipper called me over. He asked me to climb to the searchlight platform about 10 feet above the bridge, switch on and sweep the light along the Mole - a must unusual thing, for we never had to show the merest flicker at sea. He said count to five, switch off and get down. I think I counted to about three and was down before the light went out.

'Obviously we were meant to be seen and the skipper rang down for full speed as one shore battery after another opened fire. The Special Officer was standing at the binnacle, calling out the bearings to his colleagues who charted the gun flashes, and we ran along the French coast for about an hour.

'As they left the ship the following morning, I heard them say to the skipper 'These will be with the Air Ministry this afternoon.' So, obviously, the gun batteries were to be bombed on D-Day. We returned to our base in Portland and saw hundreds of tanks, guns and lorries lined up on Chesil Beach ready for embarking into the landing craft.

'On June 4, our flotilla sailed and were to escort 10 rather large American infantry craft to a place called Omaha Beach to arrive at 0630. Because of the weather and the problems for the smaller craft, we were recalled.

'Next day, June 5, we were called at 0700. Little did we realise this was the last sleep we were to get for the next 72 hours or so. We sailed again at three in the afternoon, formed up our charges into two columns of five, and, as Senior Officer, we were at the head and placed one of our flotilla on the outside of each column and one at the rear. Our ETA was to be 0630 at Omaha on June 6.

'As daylight broke, we sailed through the lines of battleships. On our starboard side was USS Augusta, while further to starboard was USS Nevada, which had been sunk at Pearl Harbour and re-floated to take part in the bombardment which started a few minutes after we had passed through.

'To hear these enormous projectiles whizzing over us was absolute bedlam and to me, a 19-year-old, very frightening. The barrage lifted at 0625 and a few minutes later, the ships we had escorted started to discharge their men. The next hour or so was frenzy and chaotic. It was sad to see so many dead and dying unable to get across the beach.

'Being so close in, we could see where the fire was coming from on the cliffs and sand-dunes and signalled for permission to open fire, but received negative - 'you may hit our own men.' 'We were ordered instead to make a smoke screen along the beach to give protection to the next wave of troops. At about 10am, the situation was becoming desperate and we were then requested to open fire, which the four of us did from about 700 yards. We returned to England - only to prepare for the invasion of Walcheren in the Sheldt estuary, where a very good friend from Radcliffe was killed. Will man never learn the futility of war?"

Bill Netherwood with his comrades

I sewed the medals on dead bodies

"We joined a queue of about 10,000 soldiers lining up to be shelled and killed, basically"

Words by Terry Morgan

Retired upholsterer William (Bill) Netherwood now lives in Radcliffe, but when the war broke out, he was living and working in Ancoats, Manchester. Bill had joined the Territorial Army in 1938 when rumblings of war could already be heard, so he was immediately called up when war was declared along with the rest of the workforce at the upholstering firm he worked for.

"Everyone in the building went, apart from two people - it was quite common for that to happen."

After training in the 52nd Field Regiment in Ardwick, he was sent abroad and did not return to England until 1946. Working as an equipment repairer - a 'waxy' as they were known - and transporting ammunition for the artillery, Private Netherwood was involved in fighting in France, the Sinai Desert and Italy, and was posted in Iraq to guard the borders to Turkey to prevent 'Jerry' from attacking from the East. His views on war, and in particular its futility, are clear as he shares some of his memories.

"After most of the fighting I was involved in, I have to say I was surprised that we actually won the war. The Germans always had better equipment and firepower, and more of it, wherever we went it seemed.

'Dunkirk was carnage. To be honest, I thought 'this is it, it's all over' when we were on that beach. We joined a queue of about 10,000 soldiers lining up to be shelled and killed, basically.

Being in the artillery, we knew exactly how long it would take for a shell to be sent over and when they would hit, but most of the soldiers didn't and so many just ran into the sea. I'll never forget that sight - just hundreds of soldiers in the water, alive and dead. Most of them were under 21 years old.

'We were caught completely on the hop after the French and Belgian front had collapsed, cut off with no equipment, nothing. That day would have put the wind up the most courageous of soldiers."

But he does recall how the Navy saved many of them that day.

"They were marvellous at Dunkirk. I'll always remember one of the Naval Officers stood on the wooden platform we were dropped onto when it was our turn. He was a high-ranking officer, but he stopped amid all the shelling to warn us about the holes in the platform made by the bombs and not to fall through them.

I've never forgotten that." Most of the memories of war are still very clear and vivid for Mr Netherwood, now aged 88.

"These days, I'll sometimes forget what I had for dinner but I can remember some of those times 60 years ago like they were yesterday. And I'll never forget my Army number. I doubt many soldiers have.

We knew it quicker than we knew our own name."

In the Italian campaign, Bill and his unit spent time in Rome, Florence and Naples, where the soldiers "had to put up with three weeks of solid rain. It was so grim - it was the only time we were issued a rum ration."

An experience which remains horribly fresh in his mind is the Battle at Monte Cassino in Italy, which was heavily bombed several times in the summer of 1944.

"There were at least 200 planes overhead, dropping bomb after bomb.

At the end of the attack, the place was just a mess, rubble. I was sent in to clear up the casualties, and for several hours, my job was to sew the medals onto dead bodies.

That was perhaps one of the worst things I had to do."

It is evident that such experiences are not those that Mr Netherwood likes to speak of, but he believes it is important for today's generation to understand what war is about.

"The reality of war is something that ought to be drummed into youngsters today - it's killing people - that's more or less all it is. Around 105,000 soldiers died in Italy - a huge number. The whole thing was a terrible business.

I was one of the lucky ones."

Bill did not come out of the war physically unscathed however; he returned home partially deaf and remains so today "due to the bombs," and "all the time I spent in and out of the gun-pit, delivering ammo. The noise was incredible."

Although there were few good times to be had. A few memories make Bill smile, such as dancing with Italian girls in Sienna while on leave there, where they also saw the King who visited the boys at the front line.

A small ambition was also achieved in seeing the Leaning Tower of Pisa when his unit passed through on the way to Rome.

"We couldn't leave the vehicles to have a proper look, but at least I got close!

'I read about the war in Iraq today and I just think if any of those in charge nowadays had experienced what we did 60 years ago, they wouldn't be hurrying back into another one. There's no justice in any war, and it's always the innocent who do the suffering. I just wish people would realise that."

Bill during the war years

Cold-blooded murder!

A report from the Bury Times dated May 12, 1945

Words by Terry Morgan

Reverend Eric Bertram Jones, the senior chaplain of Stalag Luft III prison camp, where 50 RAF Officers were shot last year, said: "Their deaths were nothing but cold-blooded murder."

Liberated by the Guards Armoured Division while in hospital in Germany, the 38-year-old was now with his wife and family at his home in Walmersley Road, Bury.

He said: "I have facts from the men who escaped with the 50 murder officers. They were all rounded up, put in gaols all over Germany and then taken out of their cells and shot in cold blood.

'I spent a long time trying to recover their bodies. We argued with the German authorities and made representations to all sorts of people. Finally, we were given 50 small tins, in which the Germans said were ashes of the officers. I signed the burial certificate, and on December 4, I interred them in a cemetery built by RAF Officers outside the camp.

'The 50 officers were given a lovely grey granite resting place, beautifully designed by officers in the camp, and with scrolls on the top giving their names and the crest and motto of the RAF.

'At the service, we placed a wreath there from the 11,000 men in the camp. The Germans had bought it for us."

The POW camp and the mass escape - and murder - of the RAF Officers was immortalised in the classic war film, The Great Escape, starring Steve McQueen, Richard Attenborough, James Garner, Charles Bronson and Donald Pleasance.

Reverend Eric Bertram Jones

I thought, 'this is me, done'

"We would stand there naked and shivering while Dr Mengele picked out people he wanted to be murdered by gassing"

Words by Karen Openshaw

To look at Mayer Hersh, one would never guess at the atrocities he has experienced in his life. He is smartly dressed, softly spoken and impeccably mannered.

But his gentle exterior masks a history of suffering - as an individual, as part of a family, as part of a nation.

Amazingly, Mayer survived the Holocaust and he is the only one of his 100-strong extended family from Poland who has lived to tell the tale.

Now living in the borough, Mayer's memories - at the age of 77 - are still as vivid as they were more than 60 years ago, and thanks to the book Beyond the Gates of Hell by Colin Rushton, they will be remembered forever.

Mayer's living nightmare began when he was 13 and living with his parents, four brothers and sister in the small town of Sieradz in Western Poland.

His older brother Jacob had already been taken to a slave labour camp at Rawcz and Mayer's father correctly predicted that he would be next.

He said: "They came in the middle of the night. It was March 1940. There was a knock at the door by a soldier and a policeman. My name was shouted and I was ordered to get dressed immediately. My mother got out of bed to help me get ready and collect some things she thought might be useful, like a prayer book and some clothing. I never said goodbye to my father or brothers and sisters. My mother hugged and kissed me and she had tears in her eyes. I wondered if we would ever see each other again. We didn't."

Mayer was taken to a slave labour camp by cattle truck. He learned later that his family had been murdered. His mother and three brothers were taken to a nearby convent where they were kept for five days without food or water. From there, they were taken in gassing vans where their fate was inevitable.

Mayer's father was gassed on arrival at Auschwitz.

German records showed that the average survival time for a Jew in Auschwitz was no more than 12 weeks. Amazingly, Mayer lasted 18 months.

The young boy, who was liberated on the last day of the war aged just 18, survived nine concentration camps in total.

How he managed to stay alive is still a mystery to him to this very day.

"I don't know why I survived," he said. "I really don't. Perhaps it was luck and because I had a strong faith. I was young and naive and I was day-dreaming all the time that one day I would go back to my family. I was not unique, no different to anybody else, but many others were too cynical and realistic."

Mayer said some people died after liberation in hospital simply because they believed they had no family left to go home to.

If it was optimism that kept Mayer alive, he must have had plenty of it.

He said: "There were many ways you could die - from starvation, extreme hard work or brutal beatings. There were also the Dr Mengele selections where he would pick out people he wanted to be murdered by gassing. We would stand naked and shivering while he selected who he wanted." Mayer survived 40 such occasions.

Another incident where he thought certain death was to follow was when he was picked on by a drunken SS man.

He said: "One day, I was scrubbing the floor in the barracks when a drunken SS man came in. He called out to me 'You.' I got up and he took me outside. We didn't argue with a sober SS man, never mind a drunken one. I couldn't plead with him. He took out his pistol and I thought 'this is me, done.' All of a sudden, he said 'Halt!' and ordered me back to the barracks. He took off his belt and gave me 10 strokes. It was just sport to them, enjoyment. I knew I was alive because I could feel the pain. That was the test.

'Only once did I reach the end of my tether. I could not see any hope. It was March 1945, on a death march. We were deprived of food and had to march for days. Anyone who stopped would be shot straight away. We had been marching for some days and I had no more energy left. We had to go over mountainous terrain. I could see no point in demeaning myself any longer. But only half of myself decided that. I spoke my thoughts aloud and my colleagues said I could not give up now - the war was almost over. Complete strangers saved my life."

Even when Mayer was liberated, he was close to death suffering from typhus and weighing barely four stone. He was taken straight from the camp to a hospital in Prague.

"I hadn't seen hot water or soap for five years," he said. "If I was dirty, it was an understatement. But as soon as I was clean, I felt better. Whether it was psychological or not,

Mayer Hersh today

I don't know."

Mayer's strength of mind has clearly contributed to his survival and he has equally strong views about not letting history repeat itself.

He said: "I wouldn't want any human being to go through what I went through. I have contributed to this book so we can learn something from it and also as a tribute to the memory of my family and community who were murdered by human wickedness. The murderers not only wanted to kill our people but wanted to wipe out their memory as well. If we are going to be bystanders and indifferent, then we are encouraging it."

Sadly, Mayer's brother Jacob, his only surviving relative, died last year, which he described as feeling like his whole family had died again.

"We owe it to the world to be a witness to the barbarity that happened to our people," he said.

Beyond the Gates of Hell is published by Mediaworld/Best Books.

Contact www.mediaworldnews.co.uk for details.

What you are capable of doing when you have no other choice...

"We ran like hell obviously, it's not like we were there to sunbathe!"

Words by Alison Barton

Nobody wins a war, nobody! That was the opinion of Whitefield man Captain Jack Wallis, who fought with the Lancashire Fusiliers throughout the Second World War - during both the Dunkirk and Normandy (D-Day) landings in France and remained in Germany after the war's end to disband the Nazi Army. Captain Wallis, who lived in Ferndale Avenue, made the journey back to France 10 years ago for the 50th anniversary commemoration of D-Day.

He was joined by his younger brother Harold - a driver with the Irish Guards during the war - and 1,600 Allied veterans, widows and relatives on the Canberra as part of the flotilla that made the pilgrimage back.

The reunion was "unbelievably moving" for the veterans, reflected Capt Wallis - going back to the Normandy beach that was the scene of their shared conflict.

"It was incredible to see 10,000 old men with hunched backs straighten up when the band played. It took 20 years off them and brought all the memories flooding back."

Captain Wallis, who was aged 85*, remembered the chaos of the day he and his men reached the beaches at Arromanches near Normandy.

"We travelled on an American landing craft. The idea was to get as close to the beach as possible but we were dropped six foot from the shore. What we didn't know was that the beach shelved deeply and we were up to our necks. Some men even began floating away. I was in charge of 30 men, so there was no time to be frightened - the responsibility drove away the fear."

'It is amazing what you can experience and not take into account what it is you're going through until later on, in retrospect," agreed Mrs Wallis, the Captain's wife of 62 years. She worked as an Air Raid Warden in Manchester and recalled shocking scenes during the Blitz there.

"You just had to get on with it. The war years really made you realise what you are capable of doing when you have no other choice."

After he returned home in 1946, Captain Wallis rarely talked about what he experienced during his military tenure, partly as a habit - he was

Captain Jack Wallis

responsible for censoring his mens' letters home - but largely because of the difficulty in describing such harrowing times.

It was during his time in Germany while tracing down Nazi soldiers that Captain Wallis played a part in discovering the Bergen-Belsen camp near to their Hanover base.

He went there with some other Army members and the British reporter who had made the request that they go there.

He was not allowed to enter the camp due to the risk of typhoid, but Captain Wallis kept the photographs the reporter took of the camp - photographs that were not published to the public until many years later due to the sensitive issues surrounding the Final Solution. "It is an experience I will never forget."

As something of a survival mechanism, Captain Wallis and the rest of the men shared a laugh and a joke whenever possible. It was essential to be light-hearted at times to cope with all the suffering they witnessed and went through themselves.

The humour was still very much present at the 50th commemoration.

Captain Wallis remembered a reporter asking a Lancashire veteran what the soldiers did when they got to the shore.

The quick reply was: "We ran like hell, obviously, it's not like we were there to sunbathe!"

Strong friendships were forged during the war, as camaraderie was extremely important for the men's morale.

Captain Wallis joined up with two other pals, Tommy Stuart and Cyril Pundick.

"We did have some fun times, the three of us together," and he kept in close touch with a number of his comrades.

War was a great leveller, and graves of men of all faiths are lined up side by side at Bayeux War Cemetery, where Captain Wallis and his brother also visited in 1995.

Many of his colleagues are buried there and he laid Stars of David with poppies attached onto the graves of Jewish soldiers. "There was no anti-Semitism there," said the Captain.

Captain Wallis talked of the futility of war. The Allies may have won, but it was a hollow victory in his opinion.

War has no victors, only countless sufferers.

*Sadly, since this interview was carried out, Captain Jack Wallis has passed away.

The day the heavens came down on Chapel Street...

"Three-piece suites were in the trees and there was glass everywhere"

Words by Terry Morgan

Just before six o'clock on the morning of Christmas Eve, 1944, a Doodlebug bomb fell on Chapel Street, Tottington. It wrecked a row of terraced houses and killed six people. Several injured were taken to Bury General Hospital, and one later died from her injuries. As often happens, fate played strange tricks. Two of the dead were Mr and Mrs James and Teresa Dyson of Nottinghamshire. They had arrived only the day before to spend Christmas with Mrs Dyson's sister, who was spared because she was a nurse on night shift when the bomb fell. The Bury Times reported: "Two of the first rescuers on the scene were local constable PC Lovatt and vicar Reverend H.W. Rogers. Lovatt rescued a man and his wife whose cottage was partly demolished.

'Rescue services were soon on the scene but several hours had passed before the last body was recovered from under the wreckage. The nearby church suffered damage from blast and flying debris. All the windows, except one behind the altar, which singularly only recently had its bomb protection cover removed, were blown out, but the Christmas services were held as usual.

'The churchyard trees were littered with smashed furniture and articles of clothing." On the site today stands a memorial garden with a plaque to the dead: Nicholas Conway, aged 50, and his wife Mary; Elizabeth Draper, aged 56, shop assistant; James and Teresa Dyson, Ann Greenhalgh, aged 75, and Bertha Greenhalgh.

Former Tottington Councillor Bill Johnson was 22 when the bomb fell. He lived with his parents and sister at Clay Butts Farm in Cann Street, Tottington.

He recalls: "It was when most of the wartime restrictions were relaxed. Lighting was kept on all night. The element of danger for bombing had passed. No one expected we would be hit by Doodlebugs.

'I remember hearing this thing coming, standing in the farmyard. Then there was an almighty flash and bang. It was horrendous. The sad thing about the bombing was that people had

Former Tottington Councillor Bill Johnson was 22 when the bomb fell

come to the quiet backwater of Tottington from the south of England to stay with relatives over Christmas, only to be killed by the Doodlebug.
'If it had landed one or two hundred yards farther on, it would have landed in a field and no one would have been killed. If it had landed short, it would have totally destroyed the town centre."

Bill and his father William were working on the farm when they heard an explosion.

"We had all our cattle tethered with rope and always carried a knife with us. If a bomb dropped on us, we could at least cut the animals free.

'Me and my father stood in the yard after hearing a bomb fall in Radcliffe. We were

mesmerised - wondering what was happening. We then heard this almighty bang and flash. We could hear falling masonry and people shouting. It was catastrophic. Our farm is far away from the town centre, up on the hillside. Yet the force of the blast took out several windows. It was a tremendous blast.

'The people who lived on Turton Road came out that morning. They were in shock. It was a terrible sight to see. To see the devastation, it was a miracle the church was not totally destroyed. Three-piece suites were in the trees and there was glass everywhere."

HITLER'S V-WEAPONS

THE German buzz bomb of 1944 was a triumph of design.

Although too late to affect the course of the war, it diverted guns and fighter planes away from the Allied offensive in Normandy. Pilotless and costing only about the same as a Volkswagen, the V1 flying bomb, or Doodlebug, could deliver nearly 2000lb of high explosive to a target, although not very accurately.

Design was crude. Fuel was force-fed by compressed air to a simple jet engine. Navigation was by compass bearing and distance.

When the planned flight time was up, a detonator put the bomb into a dive. This would usually stop the motor too. Flight corrections were by gyro-controlled rudder and elevators. There were no ailerons. If a wing dropped, it was picked up by a twitch of opposite rudder. Perhaps the bomb's greatest effect was on morale. When the motor cut out, everyone on the ground would dive for cover. This not only disrupted the war effort, it was also hard on the nerves.

Because of limited range, the V1s used in the attacks on Manchester were air-launched. Heinkel 111 twin-engined bombers flew to a point off the Yorkshire coast, each with a V1 buzz bomb slung underneath.

The V in V1 is not for 'victory,' but for the German word for 'reprisal' - vergeltung.

A 'German' soldier guards the railway crossing at Bolton Street Station
Right: ELR Wartime Weekend attracts re-enactment enthusiasts from across the country

Sacrifice will never be forgotten

"Re-enactment as commemoration has been quietly growing in popularity"

Words by Deborah Lewis

The numbers of surviving ex-servicemen and women who fought in the war may be falling, but the practice of honouring those who made the ultimate sacrifice is alive and well. The Ministry of Defence commemoration of the Second World War in July will be the last, official, formal, publicly funded event held. Minister for Veterans, Ivor Caplin, has said of the occasion: "Sixty years have passed since those final shots were fired, and although this will be the last official commemoration of the Second World War, the fortitude shown and sacrifice made by so many at home and around the world will never be forgotten." This is a sentiment that is shared by many people across the UK, not least by a growing

number in Bury. For some time now, re-enactment as commemoration has been quietly growing in popularity, and Bury is something of a key area of the country for enthusiasts. Bury businessman Keith Broome is one local devotee.

A member of the Military Vehicle Trust (MVT) for 27 years, Keith, aged 54, is now the main sponsor of the East Lancashire Railway (ELR) Wartime Weekend, which is held every year at Bolton Street Station in Bury.

Keith, who owns Purr-O-Lux at Albion Mill Creative Living Furniture Warehouse on Albion Street, was one of the very first members of the MVT when it was founded in 1969 for a growing number of military vehicle fans and experts.

It is now the UK's largest club of its kind, a charitable organisation with over 5,500 members worldwide.

As the owner of 13 military trucks, jeeps and motorcycles, many of which he has restored himself, Keith remains as passionate about his hobby now as the day he started, and provides essential support to the ELR Wartime Weekend - now the biggest event of its kind in the country.

"The whole re-enactment and remembrance scene is going from strength to strength," said Keith.

"It is something that attracts people of all ages and from all walks of life. I've met so many different people through MVT and its associations, many of whom I meet up with regularly at events."

Fellow Bury man Barrie Ryan has been friends with Keith for more than 20 years after meeting through MVT, and it is clear where their common interests lie.

Barrie owns and runs Platoon, a shop that sells all manner of vintage wartime clothing, accessories and war paraphernalia.

He met Keith through the MVT and moved his business to Bury from Manchester in 2001, when Keith offered him premises in the Albion Mill, downstairs from his furniture warehouse.

Barrie, aged 54, is another lifelong fan of militaria - "ever since I discovered soldiers when I was 10!" - and started the business more than 15 years ago when he was frustrated with the increasing lack of authentic military gear in Army and Navy stores.

Since then, he has amassed an impressive amount of vintage collectable goods. Platoon is like an Aladdin's cave of military and historical wares. And there is certainly a high demand for it. Barrie relies largely on word of mouth to boost custom, as his is the only business of its kind in the Bury area.

"Surplus wear is still of course very popular for its original function of outdoor clothing, and more recently, as fashion items," said Barrie. "But most of my custom comes from people looking for wartime uniforms and 1940s civilian dress for re-enactment purposes."

Keeping the memories of the war alive, both on the home and fighting fronts, is a philosophy that an increasing number of people clearly subscribe to.

Neil Parkington is the man behind the ELR's Wartime Weekend, which is now in its seventh year.

The 58-year-old retired caretaker used to organise 1960s events, but was asked by the ELR to be events co-ordinator for its first 1940s weekend.

He has not looked back since, and now spends nine months of every year organising the event, which includes a victory ball, a re-enactment battle, a military parade and a fashion parade and numerous stands and stalls.

"The whole 1940s war era has become a big business, and interest and enthusiasm for it show no signs of slowing," said Neil. The Wartime Weekend, held over the Bank Holiday weekend at the end of May, attracts well in excess of 5,000 visitors from all over the country - and abroad - each year. Such is its popularity that some participants camp out in Irwell Vale because all hotels are fully booked!"

Although the event is open to everybody, it is one of the main events on wartime and military enthusiasts' calendars, as well as war veterans, and many attend in authentic period dress.

"People bring all sorts of things - even tanks!" said Neil.

Indeed, Keith Broome takes along a number of his vehicles for display at the ELR every

year, as he does to around 15 other similar events held around the country such as the annual Yanks Event in Saddleworth.

Neil, who is also involved in an online guide called Friends of the 40s, said the motivation behind the continuing enthusiasm is to make sure future generations do not forget about the country's past, and also learn from it.

"These sorts of events are like living history and a way of passing on its lessons," he said. Re-enactment is an appealing way for young people to be taught history - something that can be witnessed, touched and worn rather than just read about.

"Lots of families come to the events," agreed Keith.

"It's a great day out, educational as well as fun, and something that they can all enjoy together - and there are not too many things like that these days."

This is another salient reason for the popularity of the war period; many are nostalgic for the strong community spirit that characterised the Home Front, as well as the military camaraderie.

The Home Front was all about 'doing your bit' for a common good and sticking together, an ethos which is noticeably lacking in society nowadays. There was a feeling of safety in a united war effort, a feeling that is, paradoxically, rarely felt in these days of relative peace.

While the longer spectacles like Wartime Weekends are key events in the year, dances and other social happenings dedicated to the era are held almost every week by different groups and individuals up and down the country.

"If you had the time and inclination, you could almost indulge in the hobby full-time!" said Neil. The social side of re-enactment is another of its essential facets, and one that

keeps many coming back. A great number of people value the chance to meet other like-minded people to reminisce, chat and make new friends, and more often than not, have fun on the dance floor.

Jive bands and groups are very popular at the regular dances, at which everybody must be wearing authentic 1940s attire (either civilian or military) by strict requirement. Accuracy in clothes and uniforms and knowledge of the era is very important to the re-enactors, many of whom spend a lot of time and money. Some of the collectable helmets in Barrie's shop go for upwards of £1,000 in getting things exactly right. An exacting accuracy is particularly important at those re-enactment events attended by ex-servicemen and women, as there is no doubt any mistake will be spotted by them.

"A number of times I've heard a veteran giving a re-enactor a ticking-off for getting the uniform or equipment wrong," said Neil. "They really appreciate it when they see younger people making such efforts to get it right, but they certainly don't hesitate to tell them if it's wrong."

Therefore, people take up the hobby of re-enactment for a variety of different reasons - to honour, to learn, to socialise, to dance, to share memories, to share collections, to do something completely different and to escape the modern world. And thanks to its popularity with people of all ages, there seems a good chance it will continue long into the future.

Neil described the people who regularly attend the commemoration events as "a wonderful crowd."

"Really, it is the people who make it what it is," he added.

In many ways, the same could be said of those who lived through the war 60 years ago.

The silver torpedo monument at Whitehead Gardens, Bury

The courage of the 'Little ships'

"Such heroism had a price and by the war's end, 1,024 ratings had been killed along with 148 officers"

Words by Lynsey Southall

A national war memorial paying tribute to the Navy's 'little ships' is sited in Bury. The silver torpedo monument commemorates the 1,172 men who died defending the coast of Britain throughout the Second World War. Bury was chosen to receive the memorial because of the town's association with Robert Whitehead, who invented the self-propelled torpedo in the 19th century. The weapon helped the Coastal Forces (CF) sink 800 enemy vessels - including 48 E Boats - between Dunkirk in 1940 to VE Day. The torpedo memorial was sited in Whitehead Gardens to remind people about the important role the Coastal Forces played.

They were affectionately known as the Navy's 'little ships' and operated from Norway to the Aegean.

Motor torpedo boats, motor gunboats and motor launches of the Coastal Forces all served with distinction throughout the Second World War.

Of 81 enemy midget submarines destroyed, 32 were claimed by the CF. Having fired 11,069 of the torpedoes invented by Robert Whitehead, their percentage hits outstripped that of the submarine service.

Also, 32 enemy aircraft were shot down and twice as many mine-laying operations were carried out.

As a result, more than 3,000 decorations went to CF, including two VCs.

But such heroism had a price and by the war's end, 1,024 ratings had been killed along with 148 officers.

It is no coincidence that Whitehead Gardens was chosen to locate the memorial because the site, as the name implies, also has strong associations with the Whitehead family.

Robert's brother, Henry, was the benefactor who created the gardens in memory of his brother, Walter, who was a president of the British Medical Association, but was also one of the best-known surgeons in Europe.

Film fans will be interested to know that Robert's daughter, Agatha, was the grandmother of the Von Trapp children, whose escapades were featured in the film The Sound of Music.

How the world plunged back into war...

Hitler's Germany threatens peace in Europe

Words by Alan Domville

The 1930s were a time of great contrast in Britain. They began with millions of workers in the industrial north and midlands - laid off as a consequence of the worldwide economic downturn - and ended with the mobilisation of both men and women into the fighting force that would ultimately repel and defeat the powers of evil.

From the turmoil of National Government and the comfortable pacifism subsequently embraced by our leadership, the scene was set for the re-emergence of a largely forgotten man who would lead Britain and the world out of the darkness.

The monarchy had been rocked to its foundations by the abdication of King Edward VIII over his relationship with Mrs Wallis Warfield Simpson. It was a hesitant, stuttering

King George VI and his wife Queen Elizabeth who would inherit the challenge of restoring its position as head of the greatest empire the world had ever seen - on which the sun never set.

In reality, at the heart of this colossus, for most people, wages were low and job security was minimal. Doctor's bills were high but cures were few.

The Jarrow marchers, who walked from the north east to London to plead for work, and to whom the Government of the day turned a blind eye, was one of the most telling images of the early 1930s. For solace, there was always the world of sport - but there were contrasts there too.

On the cricket field, the 1930s began with the threat of the greatest schism in the world game - created by the "bodyline" bowling style of Harold Larwood. But it would be made more memorable by batsmen - the Australian Donald Bradman who hit a world test record 334 and the Yorkshireman Len Hutton who topped that in 1938 by scoring 364 at the Oval - against Australia.

In soccer, Everton, otherwise the School of Science with Dixie Dean up front, and Arsenal and Huddersfield Town, thanks to manager Herbert Chapman, were great to watch.

Rugby League, essentially the game of the cloth-capped northerner, was emerging from its heartland to take its place on the world stage with tours to the Antipodes, France and expansion into London.

But still a world apart were Wimbledon, with its strawberries and cream, Henley, awash with striped blazers and caps - and Royal Ascot, where the champagne and the dress code was far more important than the racing.

But in both the humble backyards of overcrowded terraced homes and across the greenswards of our great country houses, shadows were beginning to creep. Cars were few in Britain. It was 1935 before the driving test was introduced and 1937 before speedometers became compulsory.

Hiking, rather than driving, was the great outdoor pastime of the day - but it was the sound of marching feet in other lands that would ultimately change what had been the British way of life forever.

The code of fascism had been embraced in Germany, arising from the ashes of the First World War under a talkative, moustachioed little man called Adolf Hitler.

A despot called Benito Mussolini assumed the leadership in Italy after the fall of the monarchy and the people of Spain would be driven apart by the rival claims of the monarchists and the republicans.

But, for many people in Britain in the 1930s, Germany, Italy and Spain were far-off lands. And didn't we have a body called the League of Nations that would never again allow countries to go at war with each other? Russia, in the wake of its revolution, was surely impotent; China and Japan were surely asleep?

Codes of conduct were not nearly enough to stop Mussolini's adventure in Abyssinia in the north eastern part of Africa.

The Pact of Paris had become a dead letter because the signatory countries simply had no powers to stop the renegades among them.

And in Germany, the comical character who called himself Fuhrer no longer sounded very funny as one pledge after another was broken and re-armament was taking place at a rapid pace.

Isolationists held sway in North America. The United States also left the League of Nations, leaving it toothless.

By 1935, the Government in Britain was burying its head in the sand because it was advantageous at the ballot box. Stanley Baldwin's administration was elected on the ticket "There will be no war".

A rioter clashes with the police

Not long afterwards, Hitler had torn up the Treaty of Locarno by ordering his troops into the then demilitarised Rhineland. True, that was historically German territory - but it was a significant demonstration of Nazi power that western politicians chose to ignore. Alarm bells still weren't ringing when the National Socialists took over the German banks and the railways.

A Royal Commission investigating arms sales by British firms and privateers abroad was utterly ignored by central Government. The Conservatives didn't hold with the idea of regulating the arms manufacturers while Labour were disappointed that nationalisation remained off the agenda. And so, nothing was done. But in those very same factories, the workers were not blind to the fact that production was being increased. Fathers who had survived the horrors of the 1914-18 conflict were beginning to realise that their children could well be pitched into hostilities all over again - and this time with more sophisticated weaponry.

Could bombs really rain down on civilians in our great cities of London, Liverpool, Manchester, Coventry and Hull?

After the Italian troops marched into Abyssinia, a promising young politician called Anthony Eden told the League that ships of the British fleet would sail to the Mediterranean. Such actions were usually enough to sort things out.

But the British lion wasn't exactly roaring. Sir Samuel Hoare, the Foreign Secretary, was conceding territory to the Italians even before they had declared victory themselves.

Not surprisingly, he was soon succeeded by Eden.

But this episode was a relatively minor matter compared with what was happening in Germany, where the Nazis were stifling all opposition. In successive speeches, Hitler was railing with bitterness against the Communists to the east, the Romanies in the south and the Jews in his midst.

The 20th century's Caesar's doctrine wasn't new - indeed, he used Wagnerian legend as his inspiration - and he was using one of the then oldest tricks in the book: unite the people behind you by creating one or more common enemies.

None of this should have been any surprise; all had been revealed in his book *Mein Kampf*, hardly a gospel of the spirit of love and harmony. The Fuhrer was talking about "The Fatherland" and a race of Aryan stock - tall, fair, good looking and athletic people - with the diminutive, black-haired, unattractive and thoroughly unsporting despot at its head. Millions of Germans, motivated by his rhetoric, blinded and deafened by censorship and overwhelmed by the stage management of his performances couldn't wait to put on a uniform. Could they really be ready to die for this man?

Well they were certainly dying in Spain. Forces of democracy and those of General Franco and his fascists, of left and right, met head on in 1937 and, while non-intervention was the policy of the British and French Governments, volunteers backing each side poured into Iberia. And so too did arms.

The horrors of the battles were made real to people through the press, the radio and on the cinema newsreels. Surely the forces for good would never allow such things to happen in central Europe ever again?

In the House of Commons, the man they called the Right Honourable Gentleman Below the Gangway wondered why our own arms build-up was lagging so far behind that of Germany. Away from the public spotlight, in secret communications with the new Prime Minister, Neville Chamberlain, this "yesterday's man" of the Conservative party, was revealing the true extent of the danger that Germany were presenting. He knew, that if the truth were revealed to all, panic would set in among the British people and Germany would be even more likely to flex its muscles.

But there were danger signs all around the world. Japan had begun to build military aircraft and to make threatening noises. Russia, now called the Soviet Union, was building up its own forces too - and there were alarming reports also that, in that vast country, religions were being suppressed and intellectual liberty was being denied. Millions of dissidents were being sent to labour camps or being exterminated. Still more millions were starving.

The communist system of collective ownership had been discredited less than 20 years after the revolution - but the sinister Stalin and his cohorts were safe, ruling by fear. Once again, all had been revealed in a book written 80 years earlier by Karl Marx. *Das Kapital* had declared that a class war was inevitable and would be followed by the supremacy of the proletariat - by which he meant the party bosses. All of these things were unnerving in the minds of the ordinary man and woman in the street in Britain in 1938 - but they were still all happening far away.

- Armistice signed to end First World War
- Communist uprising in the Weimar Republic during

January 1919
- Hitler joins the German Workers' Party, 1919
- Becomes Nationalist Socialist

German Workers' Party, 1920
- Kapp Putsch fails in Berlin, March 1920
- Hitler becomes leader of Nazi

Fact file

Arthur Neville Chamberlain, pictured below, the man who made appeasement famous, was from a family of statesmen. His father, Joseph, had been leader of both the Liberal Unionist Party and then a colonial secretary in the Conservative Government. Neville himself started out in business, first managing his father's sisal plantation in the Bahamas and then moving on to a successful career in the metalworking industry in Birmingham.

It was there that he took his first political position, when he was appointed Lord Mayor of Birmingham in 1915.
He served as both Chancellor of the Exchequer (1923-24) and Minister of Health (1923, 1924-29, 1931), among other Government positions. As Minister of Health, he helped simplify social services with a series of important social reforms.
He succeeded Stanley Baldwin as Prime Minister in 1937 and the appeasement years were upon Britain.

King George VI with wife Elizabeth

At home, the real issues for most people remained those of economic survival. Unemployment still raged - the men in Jarrow were still walking the streets.
And ordinary folk wondered why seven million people who had been unemployed in Germany in 1933 when Hitler came to power were now in jobs. There was a collective feeling that Britain was no place for children. People were fearful of the future and not surprisingly, many clung to any forlorn hope that peace could be maintained.
Sir Oswald Mosley was one politician offering a solution. After drifting from credo to another, the baronet formed the British Union of Fascists, advocating that, on many issues, Hitler and Mussolini were right.
BUF meetings, which took on the aura of Nazi gatherings, became hotbeds of racial hatred and not surprisingly led to riots.
But many would go along with the cause if it meant peace. More than 20,000 enthusiastic supporters of Mosley crammed into Earl's Court Exhibition Centre, in London, in 1939.
"We want peace - and Hitler wants peace," was the drift.
Mosley was backed by many influential people - leaders in the worlds of the civil service, the military, the banks and, most importantly, the press.
The establishment's own newspaper, *The Times*, was firmly behind the appeasers,

though its finest writer, Sir Philip Gibbs, did not subscribe to the policy.
An Anglo-German Friendship Society, The Link, was founded by Admiral Sir Barry Domvile, former Commander of the Royal Yacht. His supporters included the then Duke of Westminster, Lord Redesdale, Lord Londonderry and a host of right wing MPs.
And, in a different way, pacifism was the policy of great thinkers such as Aldous Huxley, author of *Brave New World*, and Canon Dick Sheppard, one of the most influential voices in the Church of England.
Hitler was indeed offering non-aggression pacts to neighbouring countries - but who could trust a man who tore up treaties and protocols? He even suggested Germany could rejoin the League of Nations - but from a position of military strength.
One man who couldn't conceive that war was becoming inevitable was Chamberlain. In sharp disagreement with him was Eden, who resigned his post as Foreign Secretary early in 1938.
"There could be no advantage," he declared, "in shutting our eyes to events … however much we deplore them."
Eden was succeeded by Lord Halifax, a firm advocate of the peace process.
Within weeks, another broken promise by Hitler shook many of those who had hoped to avert war.
On a sunny spring morning, listeners to the BBC Home Service were informed that German troops were marching into Austria - birthplace of the Fuhrer and a country he had pledged to leave independent. That country's politicians and many of its people quickly threw in their lot with "The Fatherland" - creating what was called the Anschluss.
After years of deprivation, they wanted to be a part of the apparent economic prosperity of the German nation.
Within days, Nazi sympathisers were released from jails and were replaced by dissidents. anti-Semitic feelings spread quickly. Thuggery reigned in what had been a deeply Roman Catholic country.

party, July 1921
● Beer Hall Putsch led by Hitler fails in Munich 1923
● Hitler is tried for treason,

February 1924
● Hitler writes Mein Kampf (My Struggle) during his imprisonment

● Hitler is released from prison, Christmas 1924
● Hitler resumes leadership of Nazi Party, February 1925

In Czechoslovakia, there were more Nazi sympathisers - the impoverished minority German stock of the mountainous Sudetenland part of the country. They quickly realised a way to gain the upper hand. Czechoslovakia had been created from the ruins of the Austro-Hungarian Empire and its people was a hodge-podge of races.

Ugly incidents ensued and, within weeks, the jack-booted troops of liberation were marching into sovereign territory to the east.

Chamberlain's supporters urged the PM to keep his nerve; Labour MPs who had hitherto spoken of international solidarity now called for intervention.

Sudetenland was conceded by the Prime Minister when he travelled to Munich to meet the Nazi leadership.

And, when he landed back in Britain, he waved a piece of a paper, which he declared guaranteed "Peace with Honour" and "Peace in our Time".

Dixie Dean

His supporters in the Commons cheered him to the rafters.

In hindsight, Lord Halifax defended the initiative, saying that it had bought Britain valuable time to prepare for the worst.

By the spring of 1939, the annexation of Czechoslovakia was complete and at long last, it was clear to Chamberlain that he had been deceived.

In August, he was rocked by the announcement that the fascists of Germany and the communists of Russia had signed a peace treaty. The wily Stalin was merely following the Halifax principle of buying time, hoping that Hitler would go to war against the west.

Claiming that Polish forces had attacked Germany, and using the excuse of reclaiming land lost under the Treaty of Versailles, German forces poured into Poland on September 1, 1939. This, for Britain, was the last straw.

Poland may have been a long way off, but that country had been promised by Chamberlain that Britain would defend their sovereignty.

A note was sent by Chamberlain to the German high command calling for the withdrawal of the invasion force.

On Sunday morning, September 3, 1939, the inevitable came. A final ultimatum had been sent to Berlin by Britain and France - withdraw the troops.

The Prime Minister, addressing the country on BBC Radio, said that if he had heard nothing before 11 o'clock that morning, a

Fact file

Benito Mussolini, pictured above with Adolf Hitler, was 'Il Duce' - the Prime Minister of Italy and an Axis European political leader. Like Hitler, he served in the First World War as a young man and dreamed of military glory in a second war to come. The two were destined to become allies.

state of war would exist between us and Germany. It was a quarter past eleven.

"I have to tell you," he said in hushed tones, "that no such undertaking has been received and that consequently, we are at war with Germany."

Within months in the House of Commons, Leo Amery, using the words of Oliver Cromwell, told a desolate Chamberlain: "In the name of God, go."

The man of peace resigned.

Two days later, the hour of the Right Honourable Gentleman Below the Gangway had come.

● Hindenburg is re-elected President, 1932
● Hindenburg pronounces that Hitler is to become Chancellor,

January 1933
● Reichstag fire, February 27, 1933
● Hitler passes the Enabling Act,

March 23, 1933

Hitler's rise to absolute power is now complete

Retreat from Dunkirk's beaches as Hitler's grip closes on Europe

Britain stands alone...

Words by Alan Domville

On the day war was declared the Right Honourable Gentleman Below the Gangway in the House of Commons was given a new job - or rather, an old job.

Winston Churchill, the forgotten man in the wilderness of British politics, was restored to the position of First Lord of the Admiralty, which he had occupied during the First World War.

The signals went out from the ships all around the empire: Winston is back!

A month earlier Churchill had travelled to France, visiting the defences of the Maginot Line and the chateau of a friend west of Paris. There, as at his home Chartwell in Kent, Winston had spent many hours painting.

He would soon have to put away his easel for a long time to come.

At the same time, members of the German high command including Erich von Manstein and Franz Halder were planning the defeat of the French Army. The Manstein plan would take the German forces through Belgium, away from the Maginot Line, and directly to the North Sea coast.

Nothing happened until May 10 - the very day that Winston was asked by George VI to accept the post of Prime Minister.

The Luftwaffe bombed airfields in Belgium and Holland and the German Army marched into Rotterdam.

The French were ordered into Holland while the German Seventh Panzer Division led by Erwin Rommel, the 19th Corps commanded by Heinz Guderian and the Sixth and Eighth Panzers led by Gerd von Rundstedt poured into the Ardennes, north of the Maginot Line which the French thought to be impassable by tanks.

They were wrong. More than 2,500 of them found a way through and Paris fell two days later. Devastated by bombing raids, the Netherlands collapsed only two days later. Queen Wilhelmina, the Dutch royal family and their government escaped to London.

Apart from two battles of brave resistance by the French troops commanded by Charles De Gaulle the German forces were unstoppable. De Gaulle, in fact, had been the only French commander to make any sort of impact against the invaders. Soon afterwards he was made Minister for War.

The Belgians were next to surrender on May 28. King Leopold was arrested but members of his government were able to escape across the North Sea.

Three hundred thousand members of the British Expeditionary Force, which had been sent to France in September of the previous year with little in the way of firepower, were now in grave danger.

Eighteen days after taking power, Winston Churchill was now feeling loneliness of a different kind to that which he had experienced throughout the 1930s.

Europe was collapsing and only he and the British people could now prevent the complete domination of the continent by the evil dictator Adolf Hitler.

Churchill's first act was to call for the implementation of Operation Dynamo which had been drawn up by General John Gort, commander of the BEF "for use if necessary". This was to evacuate the troops and their weaponry from the port of Dunkirk on the northern coast of France.

The fact that they had any chance of getting away at all was due to a difference of opinion between von Rundstedt and Guderian. Hitler accepted von Rundstedt's suggestion that the tanks should wait for their infantry to catch them up before taking on the allied troops. It bought valuable time for the allies - but the evacuation remains one of the most stunning acts of rescue in history. The logistics and statistics were astonishing.

Over a period of nine days almost 700 vessels of all kinds, many skippered by volunteers, were used to bring back more than 300,000 of our troops and members of the French Army.

Thirty nine destroyers, 36 minesweepers, 77 trawlers, 26 yachts and scores of small craft plied the Channel. Under fire from the Germans, many of the soldiers and marines had to swim out to the craft to save their lives.

Erich von Manstein

ON THE RETREAT
May 1940
10 - Adolf Hitler arrives at his bunker near Aachen to direct operation Fall Gelb (case yellow) - the attack on western Europe. German forces begin Operation Sichelschnitt (sickle cut), a surprise assault against Holland, Luxembourg, Belgium, and France. Luftwaffe takes off to attack western Europe

Franz Halder

There was no chance of saving the valuable weaponry and equipment; it simply had to be abandoned.

The remaining French fighting forces led by General Maxime Weygand, Supreme Allied Commander, battled desperately to hold their positions along the Somme and Aisne rivers. Completely outnumbered, they withdrew to the Loire.

Nazi forces jackbooted their way into the centre of Paris on June 14, marching beneath the Arc de Triomphe.

Paul Reynaud, the diminutive French prime minister, was ordered to leave his desk and the wretched Henry-Phillipe Petain, who embraced the invading power and its terms for peace with sickening haste, was installed as Reynaud's successor.

Petain had served in the First World War and as Minister for War in the years that followed. He was 83 when he took over as the puppet leader. It was only his age that saved him from being executed years later after he had been brought back from Switzerland to where he had fled after the Normandy invasion.

The terms of the French surrender were agreed in the same railway carriage in which Marshal Foch had accepted the German surrender in 1918 and it was then removed to Berlin. It was a neat piece of theatre orchestrated by Hitler. The northern part of France and regions north of Vichy all came under German occupation. Petain's administration moved the seat of government to Vichy.

One of Petain's great supporters was Francois Mitterand, future President of France - but when Pierre Laval ordered Frenchmen to work in Germany in exchange for prisoners of war he broke with the Vichy administration and joined the Resistance.

One of Petain's first acts was to appropriate all of the money belonging to the professional French Rugby League because of its links with Britain, turning it over to the "more co-operative" Rugby Union who had been isolated before the war by the authorities at Twickenham for payment illegalities.

If collaboration with the enemy wasn't bad enough Petain was also turning his back on the nearly two million French soldiers who had been taken prisoner. And almost 400,000 of his countrymen had died in the fight for freedom.

Laval had become infamous in the 1930s when he and Samuel Hoare, the then British Foreign Secretary, had drawn up a plan allowing Italy to retain lands that it had conquered - a plan that led to them both being thrown out of office.

Laval urged closer ties with Hitler, backed the Gestapo looking for members of the French Resistance and deported Jews to Germany. Not surprisingly, he would face a firing squad in Paris five years later.

De Gaulle had been visiting England when Petain came to power and, fearful of being arrested on his return home, he decided to stay in London and later Algeria and lead the fight for his country's freedom from there. Many years later De Gaulle would establish the French Fifth Republic and become its first President.

The Algerian-born writer Albert Camus, who would one day win the Nobel prize for literature, joined forces with Jean Paul Satre to publish a newspaper for the Resistance called *Combat*. Also involved in the clandestine enterprise was the teacher and writer Simone de Beauvoir.

Churchill's administration was a coalition of unlikely membership. His deputy, not actually called deputy Prime Minister for another couple of years, was the untried and unassuming intellectual Clement Attlee who had taken over the leadership of the Labour Party five

Gerd von Rundstedt

13 - Churchill asks Roosevelt for assistance

15 - The Dutch King surrenders Holland to Germany. Reynaud asks Churchill for troops and planes to be sent

17 - British bombers make their first attack on Hamburg

18 - German forces capture the cities of Antwerp, St Quentin and Perrone on the Somme

20 - German forces reach the sea

Fact file

Charles de Gaulle was born on November 22, 1890 in Lille, France. A lifetime military man, de Gaulle was a Prisoner Of War during the First World War. He was Minister for National Defence and War in June 1940 when France capitulated to Germany. De Gaulle escaped to Britain, where he made a famous

broadcast calling on the French people to resist (earning him the nickname of the 'Man of June 18, 1940'). De Gaulle formed the Free French forces and became a symbol of the French resistance. After the war, he served as President and was a grand figurehead of France until stepping down in 1969. He died a year later of natural causes.

Troops retreat from the beaches of Dunkirk

years earlier from the ailing George Lansbury who, incidentally, was the uncle of the future famous actress Angela Lansbury.

George Lansbury believed deeply in the ethic that socialists should never fight each other and he had toured Europe urging that workers should lay down their weapons. He was giving the same message as the right wing appeasers of the day but from a totally different standpoint.

Churchill named himself Minster of Defence and into his war cabinet came Anthony Eden, soon to become Foreign Secretary in place of the appeaser Lord Halifax, Labour's Ernest Bevin, Hugh Dalton, Stafford Cripps and Herbert Morrison and the Liberal leader Sir Archibald Sinclair.

The dashing Anthony Eden, who had earlier served as Foreign Secretary in the Baldwin administration, was invariably treated by Churchill as his number two - but it was a position he would have to resign himself to for many years to come - and when his elevation

to the premiership came in the 1950s he was be almost instantly be brought down by the Suez Crisis when, as in the early part of the Second World War, the American administration distanced themselves from conflict.

Ernest Bevin, orphaned at the age of six, had been general secretary of the all-powerful Transport and General Workers' Union and had led the TGWU out of the General Strike in 1926. In the 1930s he had sided with the International Brigades in Spain along with a man who would ultimately succeed him as the union leader, Jack Jones. To get into parliament and become Minister of Labour, Bevin had to win a by-election in Wandsworth and then became responsible for motivating the country's labour force.

It was also Bevin who, in one of his first acts as a cabinet member, asked Wiliam Beveridge, a Liberal member of parliament, to look at ways of creating the welfare state when if and when peace returned.

near Abbeville - splitting Allied forces and trapping much of it in a pocket. General Maxime Weygand replaces Gamelin

21 - Enigma code is broken
22 - Churchill meets Weygand
23 - Boulogne falls to German troops who set siege to Calais

24 - Allied Expeditionary Force withdraws from Norway
25 - Germans capture Boulogne. Gort cancels a planned advance

The retreat from Dunkirk

Hugh Dalton became minister for economic warfare: he would experience his own economic battle some years later when, as Chancellor of the Exchequer, he had to resign because of a Budget leak. Dalton's long-time enemy Stafford Cripps (his successor as Chancellor) was the nephew of the socialist thinker Beatrice Webb and became both a pacifist and a Marxist - an unlikely member of a Churchill cabinet. In fact he lasted two years and was then asked to take charge of aircraft production that had been kick-started by Lord Beaverbrook. The latter, formerly Max Aitken, had been born in Canada, but settled in Great Britain and had become a Conservative MP. Morrison had also been a pacifist and leader of the London County Council; in 1935 he had lost the Labour leadership struggle with Attlee. Oddly enough it would be he who would release the fascist appeasers interned under the 18b regulations.

It was a time of paradoxes. Another Labour politician, the Welsh left winger Aneurin Bevan, was the most vociferous parliamentary critic of Chamberlain and the keenest proponent of the appointment of Churchill as leader of the coalition.

The task of turning the Beveridge plan for a national health service into reality when peace was restored would fall to Aneurin Bevan. Minister of Information for most of the war was Churchill's former parliamentary private secretary, Brendan Bracken.

One of Churchill's principal backers, Robert Boothby, trained as a bomber pilot while Harold Macmillan would ultimately serve as a member of the cabinet stationed in North Africa.

The man charged with creating the post-war education system was Richard Austen Butler whose 1944 Education Act would create the divisive 11-plus examination.

These were the men who would make the vital decisions as the war progressed.

But, towering above them all, was Churchill himself. A man who would, throughout the war, punctuate his waking hours with brief periods of sleep, and sustained, it is said, by a bottle of champagne and several large cigars every day.

He would need every ounce of resolve in 1940.

British forces were now back within the walls of the castle. The forces of evil were virtually at the drawbridge.

For the first time since 1066 the nation feared a successful invasion from across the Channel. And we had precious few resources with which to hit back.

Churchill's words in July 1940 were anything but downhearted:

"There are no grounds for supposing that more German troops can be landed in this country either from the air or across the sea than can be destroyed or captured by the strong forces at present under arms.

"The Royal Air Force is in excellent order and at the highest strength it has yet attained.

"The German Navy was never so weak, nor the British Army at home so strong as now.

"The Prime Minister expects all his Majesty's servants in high places to set an example of steadiness and resolution.

"They should check and rebuke expressions of loose and ill-digested opinion in their circles or by their subordinates.

"They should not hesitate to report, or if necessary remove, any officers or officials who are found to be consciously exercising a disturbing or depressing influence and whose talk is calculated to spread alarm and despondency.

"Thus alone they will be worthy of the fighting men who in the air, on the sea and on land have already met the enemy without any sense of being out-matched in martial qualities."

It was fighting talk and he knew he could count on the British people to respond.

There was no room for the cynicism and irreverence that would sadly pervade through British life in later years.

The first test of the great British resolve would come just eight weeks later.

Fact file

Educated at Oxford, Clement Attlee was called to the bar in 1905. His early experience as a social worker in London's East End led to his decision to give up law and devote his life to social improvement through politics. In 1907, he joined the Fabian Society and soon afterward, the Labour party.

to the south and orders his troops north to embark for England
26 - Germans capture Calais

27 - Belgium surrenders to Germany.
Evacuation of Allied troops from Dunkirk begins

June 1940

2 - Last of the British Expedition Force is evacuated from Dunkirk

Victory in the skies: The Battle of Britain

Their finest hour

Words by Alan Domville

The fall of France meant that the invasion of Britain could be expected at any time. It was ultimately learned that the German plan, called Operation Sea Lion, would involve the landing of more than 150,000 soldiers along the coast of southeast England and hundreds of vessels were assembled in the ports in France, Belgium and Germany itself. Words of assurance and inspiration were needed now more than ever before. Winston Churchill: "Let us therefore brace ourselves to our duties, and so bear ourselves that if the British Empire and Commonwealth last for a thousand years, men will still say, this was their finest hour." And…"Hitler will have to break us in this island or lose the war."

But the expected land assault never came. Once again, as in the days leading up to Dunkirk, there was disagreement among the members of the high command in Berlin. Hitler had been convinced by his Army chiefs that the Royal Air Force could inflict massive casualties on an invasion force - better to let the Luftwaffe, the German Air Force, smash the RAF first.

Hermann Goering

The Luftwaffe, established by Hermann Goering in 1935 in direct contravention of the Versailles Treaty (the settlement of the First World War), had become a formidable fighting force.

Using the skills of aircraft pioneers like Messerschmitt, Junkers and Heinkel, the German industrial machine had started to build hundreds of relatively sophisticated aeroplanes.

By June 1940, almost 3,000 aircraft were lined up on the airfields of the continental mainland and in Scandinavia ready to do battle.

The RAF had provided as much support at Dunkirk as they could but had lost almost 1,000 planes. The Germans had completely miscalculated the strength of the RAF - we had no more than 700 planes that were operational. But there were several factors that would help the underdog.

If the air battle was fought over Britain, it meant that our planes could stay in the air far longer than those of the Luftwaffe which would have to conserve fuel in order to return home. If our planes were hit, they could limp home; stricken German aircraft wouldn't be able to make it back.

We also had radar to track the incoming planes and we had the information being provided by Ultra, technology that would ultimately enable the boffins at Bletchley Park to de-code so many of the ciphers used by the enemy. At the time, however, like the Germans, we were over-estimating the power of the enemy.

The Messerschmitts were undoubtedly fine planes, but the Junkers Stuka in reality was a plodder. The Heinkels and the Dorniers also had limitations in that they couldn't carry enough weaponry.

Up against them were the tiny but highly manoeuvrable Supermarine Spitfire and the Hawker Hurricane.

Fighter Command, headed up by the fiercely independent-thinking Hugh Dowding, were hardly prepared for the battle when the first German planes headed towards southern England. They were Dornier bombers and their immediate targets were our radar stations, aircraft factories and airfields. They caused enormous damage and 22 of our planes were completely destroyed.

The Battle of Britain officially started on August 13 and it all got off to a wretched start. More than 200 of our planes were shot down and more than 100 of our pilots were killed within two weeks. Production of replacement aircraft was stepped up by the Canadian publisher Lord Beaverbrook, owner of the Daily Express and confidante of Churchill - but it couldn't keep pace with the losses. Pilots were being asked to do far more than their share of flying and were simply becoming exhausted.

By the end of the month, we were running out of both planes and available pilots.

And there was a major disagreement between divisional commanders Keith Park and Trafford Leigh-Mallory, the son of a vicar who was born in Mobberley in Cheshire.

GOERING'S DOWNFALL
- Born in Rosenheim on January 12, 1893
- Entered the German Army in 1914 as an Infantry Lieutenant before being transferred to the Air Force as a Combat Pilot
- The last Commander in 1918 of the Richthofen Fighter Squadron, Goering distinguished himself as an air ace, credited with shooting down 22 Allied

BB | WWII - An account of local stories

A Spitfire in action

bombing raid on Berlin instigated by Charles Portal, newly appointed head of Bomber Command. Goering had always assured Hitler that no bombs would ever fall on Germany. Said Winston Churchill: "Never in the field of human conflict was so much owed by so many to so few."

It certainly was the victory of the Few - in total, less than 3,000 pilots and air crew whose contribution had, for the time being at least, saved the nation. More than 500 of them had lost their lives.

Many of the pilots had come to Britain from the Commonwealth and central European countries.

Those who lived to tell the tale entered the realms of legend … Douglas Bader, Raphael Tuck et al.

The battle within the Battle of Britain - that between the strategists was resolved later in the year. Air Chief Marshal Portal appointed Douglas to take over from Dowding as head of Fighter Command. Leigh-Mallory took over Fighter Group II and Park lost his job.

Immediately after the Battle of Britain, Hitler ordered that his bombers should now aim for civilian targets. The invasion remained on hold, but now the reality of war was certainly going to be felt by the ordinary person in the street.

Liverpool and Birmingham were hit first - and then came London's turn. More than 1,000 enemy aircraft headed towards the capital on September 7 and a daylight aerial attack on the capital began.

More than 400 people were killed and almost

Park, whose responsibility was to defend the skies east of London, felt that his bases should be receiving more protection from Leigh-Mallory's squadrons.

Dowding sided with Park while Air Vice Marshal William Sholto Douglas took Leigh-Mallory's view that we should be meeting the German planes rather than waiting for them to arrive.

In the last two days of August, each side suffered heavy casualties. We shot down more than 40 enemy aircraft but they destroyed 50 of ours.

For Britain, it seemed the numbers simply weren't adding up. Just a few more days and it would all be over.

But, astonishingly, the Germans didn't realise that. Their calculations about the number of planes we had was wildly inaccurate - we were simply sending up the same aircraft time and again.

September 15 was critical, with the Germans losing scores of planes. We now know that the Luftwaffe lost almost 1,400 of their planes in total - almost twice as many as the RAF.

Hitler had been stunned by what appeared to be defeat in the aerial conflict and also by a

2,000 sustained injuries and hundreds of homes destroyed.

It happened all over again the next day with similar casualty levels. The resolve of the Londoners and the British people was now to be given its sternest test.

Fact file

On December 15, 1944, Glenn Miller boarded a single engine C-64 Norseman aircraft to travel to Paris, where he was to make arrangements for a Christmas broadcast. Tragically, the plane never reached France and was never found.
The band, without Miller, performed the scheduled Christmas concert under the direction of Jerry Gray.

aircraft. Awarded the Pour le Merite and the Iron Cross (First Class)
● Joins the Nazi Party (NSDAP)

● On March 1, 1935, he was appointed Commander-in-chief of the Air Force
● Directed the Luftwaffe

campaigns against Poland and France, and on June 19, 1940 was promoted to Reich Marshal
● In August 1940, he

Lord Beaverbrook

engineering capacity and aircraft manufacture.

Hull was an easy target. The German planes could get there quicker than anywhere else and inflict enormous damage very quickly.

Astonishingly, the Germans didn't seem to realise that by destroying the Crewe and March rail terminals they could probably have brought the country to its knees in days. Londoners took shelter deep in the ground - in the stations of the Tube, remaining there until the early morning "all-clear" was sounded. But even there, safety wasn't guaranteed when the bombs rained down.

There were direct hits on the stations in Trafalgar Square, Praed Street, Balham and Bounds Green.

Gas and electricity supplies were cut off and the shortage of food became even more acute. Canteens were set up all over the East End by Lord Woolton, the Minister of Food, and his deputy, the MP Robert Boothby.

Children were told to go to school only to collect homework.

It is now known that hundreds of thousands of paper maché coffins had been made ready for the onslaught, but they were never used.

Fear was truly real - and it seemed that only the voice of a great Englishman could maintain morale.

Churchill went into the East End and was moved to tears when he saw what his countrymen, women and children were having to endure. The King and Queen, continuing to live in the bombed Buckingham Palace, along with their daughters, would often walk amid the shambles that Stepney and Bow had become to join with the people in their hours and days of grief.

The human toll was enormous in London and across the country. More than 60,000 people were killed, half of them Londoners, almost 100,000 were injured and more than two million homes were destroyed.

For the moment, phlegmatic citizens must have felt that it was safer serving as a soldier,

sailor or airman than walking in the street. There was another voice that the British people also heard. William Joyce, broadcasting from Germany, continually urged us to surrender. He told of enormous victories that the Nazis were achieving in order to destroy the morale of the British people. In due course, Joyce would be hanged for treason.

Disappointments there certainly - but every setback seemed to strengthen the resolve of the British people more and more. Bad weather brought some respite after the turn of the year and in May 1941, after a devastating final raid on London, the Blitz (the German word for lightning) came to an end - at least for several years.

Once again, the German high command changed their tactics. An attack on Russia was being planned and, bearing in mind the experience of another man with illusions of world domination, Napoleon Bonaparte, in the previous century, Hitler knew that his assault, codenamed Barbarossa, would have to take place during the favourable weather of the summer.

German resources were switched to the eastern front, where millions would lose their lives. The protracted battle did extend into winter and on and on until February 1943 after the Battle of Stalingrad in which 150,000 people died and 45,000 German soldiers were marched off to labour camps in Siberia.

The Germans had been smashed to defeat. The tide of the war was turning.

The Battle of Britain had been won, the Blitz on our cities resisted.

The Germans were pre-occupied with the Russians and engaged in battle in the North African desert.

Covert assistance had been agreed between Britain and the United States but there was great animosity that Britain was still standing alone, defending the western way of life.

To the boys at his old school, Harrow, Churchill declared: "Never give in. Never, never, never, never, in nothing great or small, large or petty, never give in except to convictions of honour and good sense. Never yield to force; never yield to the apparently overwhelming might of the enemy."

And on December 9 1941, the Japanese attacked Pearl Harbour. The Americans, at last, were in the war for real.

During the next nine months, more than 70 such raids were endured by the people of London - with those from November onwards always being conducted at night. The East End area around the docks - home manors of the Cockneys - bore the brunt of the attacks.

Fire, falling masonry and vermin all contributed to the horror. Each morning, people were found dead or dying in the streets or in the wreckage of their homes. Broken glass seemed to be everywhere.

What was world's last bastion of democracy fighting for freedom, the House of Commons, was also hit. A huge bomb landed next to the Speaker's Chair.

So too was Buckingham Palace. "Now," said the Queen, "we can look East Enders in the face."

Even more potent was the sight one would see walking up Fleet Street and Ludgate Hill - the great cathedral of St Paul's surrounded by a halo of light created by the bombing and its destruction.

Other cities targeted were Manchester and its giant Trafford Park industrial complex in the north west, Coventry and Nottingham in the midlands, Plymouth and Bristol in the west country, Glasgow in Scotland, Sheffield in south Yorkshire, Newcastle in the north east, Hull on the east coast, Southampton and Portsmouth in the south, Cardiff in Wales and Belfast in Northern Ireland.

The great cathedral of Coventry was reduced to rubble in what the Nazis claimed to be the most sustained air raid ever undertaken in history. The city was the centre of our heavy

---

threw himself into the great offensive against Great Britain - Operation Eagle - convinced that he would drive the RAF from the

skies and secure the surrender of the British by means of the Luftwaffe alone
● On May 9, 1945, Goering was

captured
● After his trial at Nuremberg, Goering committed suicide on October 15, 1946

The Desert Campaign and the fall of Italy...

A dictator is toppled

Words by Alan Domville

More than a million Italian troops were based in Libya when the Italian fascist leader Benito Mussolini declared war on Britain and its remaining Allies in June 1940. Five Italian divisions headed towards Egypt in September where we had just 36,000 men whose principal task had been to protect the Suez Canal and the oilfields of Arabia, holding their advance at Mersa Matruh.

Despite being totally outnumbered, the British Empire forces, commanded by General Archibald Wavell, inflicted heavy casualties and the Italians were forced back 500 miles.

In January 1941, the town of Tobruk in Libya was captured by the British.

Hitler was appalled at the performance of the Italian troops and decided to take a desert initiative himself. The German high command had already formed a fighting force, the Afrika Corps, for such a campaign and it was decided immediately that these troops, commanded by the legendary Erwin Rommel, should join the battle.

Rommel enhanced his reputation by pushing the British forces out of Libya within seven days. Wavell ordered a counter-attack but it was repelled at Halfaya Pass. Wavell was then replaced by General Claude Auchinleck.

Operation Crusader, the largest operation yet launched in this theatre of war, began in November and success came within two weeks.

Rommel was forced to abandon his troops' siege of Tobruk - which had been grimly defended by the British, commanded by Lieutenant General Leslie Morshead. Assisted by reinforcements from Tripoli, Rommel counter-attacked and forced the British to retreat.

After losing control of Benghazi, the British troops dropped back to Gazala. Immediately, the Eighth Army, commanded by Lieutenant General Neil Richie, set up a fortified line and laid mines.

The Germans, although joined by the Italians, were outnumbered by the British troops but they began an offensive in May.

The master tactician Rommel proved too

Tanks go into action in the North African desert

good for Richie even though the latter had the numerical advantage. Rommel captured Sidi Muftah and soon afterwards two of the three British armoured brigades were defeated, losing many tanks, and Gazala had to be abandoned. By the summer of 1942, the German forces had re-taken Tobruk and 35,000 British troops had been taken prisoner. After taking on more arms and supplies, the Afrika Corps then marched into Egypt and by July 1942 were only 70 miles from Alexandria. A shocked Winston Churchill decided to travel to Egypt to look at the situation on the ground. Auchinleck was replaced by General Harold Alexander, and General Bernard Montgomery was also criticised, but the latter showed himself to be as indomitable as Churchill and his talent for tactical brilliance helped him to retain his position. The Eighth Army under his command would soon mount an offensive called Operation Supercharge that would throw the German high command into turmoil

and would ultimately lead to total victory in the desert. Rommel fell sick and went to Austria to recuperate - just at the moment Operation Lightfoot was set in motion by Montgomery. It was nothing less than the largest artillery action since the First World War. A raging Hitler ordered Rommel back to the desert with Supercharge now in full swing. Back on duty, Rommel soon conceded that he didn't have sufficient resources to defend Kidney Ridge and he ordered his troops to withdraw. An even more outraged Hitler over-ruled his General and ordered his men to continue fighting. It took just 24 hours for the Eighth Army to break through the German lines. A besieged Rommel finally persuaded Hitler to realise his desperate situation and the latter then agreed to the retreat.

The Germans and Italians were on the run and many prisoners were taken as the Eighth Army gave chase. Torrential rain on November 6 helped the decimated enemy troops to reach Sollum on Libya's border with Egypt.

THE FIRST BATTLE OF EL ALAMEIN
June 30, 1942 - A brave but disorganised Eighth Army is addressed by General Auchinleck, who tells them: "He (Rommel) hopes to take Egypt by bluff. Let's show him where to get off." 'Ultra' interceptions have foretold that Rommel will attack their positions at El Alamein the following day

Infantry soldiers head into the fray

Fact file

Erwin Rommel was born in Heidenheim, Germany, on November 15, 1891. He wanted to study engineering but his father disapproved. So, in 1910, he joined the German Army. By the outbreak of the First World War, Rommel had reached the rank of Lieutenant. He fought on the Western Front and in January 1915, he won the Iron Cross.

Two days later, a new Allied invasion began with troops led by General Dwight D Eisenhower pouring into Morocco and Algeria. The Battle of El Alamein proved to be decisive as far as the desert campaign was concerned; it was nothing less than the turning point of the whole war.

The Axis forces had been crushed and more than 50,000 of them were killed, injured or taken prisoner. But the forces of the Empire also suffered heavy casualties - 13,000 of them.

Tobruk was taken yet again by the British, bringing the battle of El Alamein to an end. It was the first major victory of the war and Churchill ordered that church bells all over Britain, silenced in 1939 and only to be rung in the event of invasion, should peel again.

Montgomery had joined his great adversary Rommel in the history books - and the latter was now under real pressure.

General Eisenhower's United States Army set in motion Operation Torch, initially invading Tunisia to where Rommel and his forces had retreated.

While the Eighth Army spent several weeks of the winter 1942-3 rebuilding their resources in Tripoli, General Jurgen von Arnium and Rommel decided to go back on the offensive, attacking the Allies led by General Kenneth Anderson. At Thala, in February 1943, they were forced to retreat.

Alexander was deputed to oversee matters in Tunisia while Rommel took charge of the German forces. Once again, Montgomery's Eighth Army won the hour. Rommel was in retreat again and Hitler was furious.

A month later, the German commander was ordered to return to Germany ostensibly "on health grounds" and was replaced by Arnium.

However, it was Arnium who had initially been handed the poisoned chalice.

British, Empire and United States forces totalled more than 300,000 in Tunisia and the Axis powers had less than 50,000 and were also greatly inferior in weaponry.

General George Patton was succeeded by General Omar Bradley as commander of the Second Corps and Bradley's troops were joined by Montgomery's for a massive offensive.

Early in May 1943, the British Empire forces took Tunis while the US Army captured Bizerte. It was the final stand of the Axis powers in the desert. Surrender came immediately and 150,000 soldiers were taken prisoner.

Churchill and Franklin Roosevelt, the President of the United States, meeting at Casablanca in Morocco, agreed that the next move would be to invade Sicily.

General Eisenhower was placed in overall command with Alexander, Patton and Montgomery taking charge of the Army. Naval operations were placed under Admiral Andrew Cunningham while Air Marshal Arthur Tedder was given command of our air forces.

The invasion of Sicily began on July 10 and, surprisingly, little opposition was mounted by the German and Italian forces in the north and west and Palermo fell. However, the Eighth Army was unable to prevent the evacuation of 100,00 Axis forces led by Field Marshal Albrecht Kesselring across the Messina Straits to Italy. The defeat proved to be the beginning of the end for Mussolini. The fascist coterie that had been running the country decided to change sides immediately - they officially surrendered a few weeks later - and King Victor Emmanuel dismissed their leader and he was arrested.

After the war, Rommel remained in the German Army and in 1929, he was appointed an instructor at the Infantry School in Dresden. In October 1935, he was promoted to the rank of Lieutenant Colonel and began teaching at the Potsdam War Academy. His 1937 book on infantry tactics brought him to the attention of Adolf Hitler.

JULY 1942
01 - Rommel captures 2,000 prisoners from the El Alamein 'box' but loses 18 of his 55

remaining tanks
02 - The British hold El Alamein despite heavy attacks. Rommel is now down to 26 tanks

03 - Due to exhaustion and lack of supplies, Rommel orders his German and Italian forces to suspend all

Fact file

Born in Texas in 1890 and brought up in Abilene, Kansas - Eisenhower was the third of seven sons.

He excelled in sports in high school and received an appointment to West Point. Stationed in Texas as a Second Lieutenant, he met Mamie Geneva Doud whom he married in 1916.

In his early Army career, he excelled in staff assignments, serving under Generals John J Pershing, Douglas MacArthur and Walter Krueger. After Pearl Harbour, General George C Marshall called him to Washington for a war plans assignment.

He commanded the Allied forces landing in North Africa in November 1942. On D-Day, 1944, he was Supreme Commander of the troops invading France.

Air Vice-Marshal Coningham and General Montgomery

Monument to the war dead at Tobruk

offensive operations before El Alamein and begin constructing defensive positions. Troops reduced to 13 tanks in a final effort to break through

05 - Axis troops start laying minefields in front of their positions at El Alamein

06 - Despite continuous attacks, Panzer Army Afrika manages to hold on to its positions

09 - Renewed German attacks

Troops head into conflict in Italy, 1944

With the establishment of bases in Sicily, the Allied powers began their assault on the Italian mainland in September.

On the fourth anniversary of Britain's declaration of war, the Eighth Army took Reggio and the Royal Navy and the First Parachute Division descended on Taranto.

The Germans put up stiff resistance against the United States forces at Salerno.

Hitler ordered that Mussolini be rescued. This was achieved by a detachment of airborne forces and he was flown by Otto Skorzeny to Germany. From there, Mussolini returned to northern Italy where he declared the establishment of the fascist republic of Salo.

Naples fell to the Allies on October 1 and two weeks later, what was left of the Italian administration made its own declaration of war on Germany.

Kesselring's forces withdrew south of Lazio and established the Gustav Line. This included the strategically important Monte Cassino, a Benedictine monastery at the top of a hill.

The battle that followed was one of the bloodiest of the war. Thousands of heavily armed German troops bravely defended their position and the Allies suffered many casualties.

Over the winter of 1943-4, the intense battle for Monte Cassino continued and Allied forces decided to try to take the port of Anzio in order to disrupt German communications.

The elation of desert victory was gradually dissipating as the Allied offensive faltered. The forces of the United States were replaced by those of New Zealand.

To resolve the stalemate, General Bernard Freyberg convinced Alexander that Monte Cassino should be bombed. It was a big mistake.

It was ascertained that the Germans were not in fact in the monastery - but after the damage had been inflicted, they immediately moved into the ruins and found the position easier to defend.

Not until May did the Allied breakthrough come. Two great generals, the Pole Wladyslaw Andersz and the Frenchman Alphonse Juin, directed the successful assault. A week later, Anzio also fell. Alexander told General Mark Clark to chase the enemy back, but Clark decided to do his own thing and ordered his troops into Rome, which was liberated on June 4.

The Allies then resumed the chase and in the summer and autumn, major towns like Assisi, Florence and Rimini were also taken. The onset of winter brought a temporary halt to the fighting but by the following April, with the war also going badly for the Germans in northern Europe, the battle for the freedom of Italy was being won.

It meant the end of the Salo regime. Mussolini and his mistress, Clara Petacci, fled but were captured by Italian partisans at Lake Como. They were shot and their bodies were displayed to the citizens of Milan - hanging upside down.

against the British defences at El Alamein bog down in the face of stubborn British resistance
14 - A British attack against Axis

positions to the South of El Alamein is repulsed
15 - New Zealander troops attack 'Kidney' Ridge in three

days of fighting which costs 2,600 prisoners and 115 guns captured
20 - Mussolini temporarily

General Karl Wolff and the Russian front veteran General Heinrich Vietinghoff, who had succeeded Kesselring, unconditionally surrendered their troops. The battle for Italy was over.

Rommel, back in Germany in 1944, and friends in high places knew that Hitler was incompetent and that he was losing the war. Rommel was urged to join a plot to assassinate the Fuhrer but he refused, believing that it would turn him into a martyr.

In the event, the plot failed. Claus von Stauffenberg carried a bomb in a briefcase into a meeting involving Hitler, Hermann Goering and Heinrich Himmler on July 20, 1944. It was decided to drop plans to kill Goering and Himmler at the same time.

After placing the case beneath a table, Stauffenberg excused himself to make a telephone call. The bomb exploded and four men died in the blast - but Hitler and his key

henchmen came staggering out of the building. The despot and his evil supporters had survived the attempt on their lives.

Hitler, now becoming more deranged following the catastrophic defeats in North Africa, Italy and Russia and the invasion of Normandy a month earlier, ordered that those responsible be found and rounded up.

The reprisal became slaughter on a massive scale. Almost 5,000 German nationals suspected of being involved in this and other plots to kill Hitler were subsequently murdered - with the alleged ringleaders being hanged by piano wire from meat hooks.

Hitler suspected that his legendary field commander, Erwin Rommel, had been involved in the plot and he sent two generals to visit him with an ultimatum: Poison yourself and be given a state funeral or be tried for treason.

Rommel elected to take his poisoned chalice.

The chivalrous commander, whose bravery had been displayed in two world wars and whose skill was always recognised and admired by his opponents, officially died of a brain seizure.

But now it was Hitler who was constantly looking over his shoulder, fearful that his hold on the mass of the German people was loosening. He must certainly have felt he might be heading for the same fate as Mussolini or worse: torture by the Cossacks.

The magnetism that had propelled him to the leadership 11 years earlier was fading fast. The head that had begun to grace the postage stamps of so many occupied countries was beginning to be replaced.

Mussolini and his mistress Clara Petacci

The Red Army was approaching from the east and the powers of Great Britain, its Empire and the United States were moving in from the west.

Claus von Stauffenberg

abandons his 'Victory March on Cairo' and returns to Rome
22 - Auchinleck musters 323 tanks against Rommel's 92 in

the second battle of 'Kidney' Ridge but loses 131 tanks and 2,600 men
23 - Fierce fighting continues

26 - An Australian attack at Alamein fails and the Eighth Army goes over to the defensive after taking 7,000 Axis prisoners.

A peaceful solution?

"He had no idea that within a year of the atomic bomb being dropped on Hiroshima, he would be walking the streets of the ruined city"

Words by Karen Openshaw

The dropping of the first atomic bomb on Hiroshima sent shockwaves around the world, but one local man has first-hand experience of the momentous moment in history.

VJ Day - August 14, 1945 - was the day on which the Japanese surrendered unconditionally to the Allies.

Although 22-year-old Herbert Hand was en route for Australia, he can clearly remember the day on which the Second World War finally ended.

"There was a great sense of relief when we heard the news, but there were no parties on board," recalled Mr Hand, who was a Sub Lieutenant in the Royal Navy serving aboard Adamant - a supply ship for the 4th submarine flotilla.

He had no idea that within a year of the atomic bomb being dropped on Hiroshima, he would be walking the streets of that ruined city.

Mr Hand, aged 70, of Higher Ainsworth Road, Radcliffe, and a former managing director of Elton Cop Dye Works, said: "It was a goodwill cruise through the Pacific Islands ending in Japan.

We reached there in 1946 but there was no hostility from the Japanese.

Like all defeated people, they were very conciliatory."

Wandering round the devastated streets, he was struck by the emptiness of the once bustling city.

He said: "No one knew very much about the effects of radiation at the time, so I was not particularly concerned for my safety. So far, I have not suffered."

Mr Hand, who has very firm views on the necessity of bombing, also visited Nagasaki, which did not suffer as much devastation as Hiroshima.

He said: "The dropping of the bomb was a terrible act but one that save many lives. War is terrible and it is very easy for people to condemn what happened, but I think you have to understand the mood at the time.

The established view was that it shortened the war and saved hundreds of thousands of lives in the long term because without the bomb, I doubt the Japanese would have surrendered.

'War is all about getting a peaceful solution. The bombs were terrible for the people who lived there but I also sympathise with those who were imprisoned and suffered at the hands of the Imperial Japanese Forces."

A monument to Hiroshima's many victims, killed by the atomic blast, inset

Lord Mountbatten, and his wife, Lady Mountbatten, meet Mahatma Gandhi at their house in New Delhi (1947)

The sooner we did our job, the sooner we could go home

"Even though he was the king's cousin, Lord Mountbatten told us that he was no different to us"

Words by Karen Openshaw

Fusilier Kenneth Ainsworth 4203997, now aged 91, tells his story. "I was born in Walshaw village near Bury on October 11, 1913, along with my twin brother. I was called up for national service on June 22, 1940. I married my wife Marion on June 20 by special licence. This meant we only had the weekend together before I reported to the Second Battalion Royal Welsh Fusiliers at Wrexham.

'My brother Edgar went to Scotland, to the Highland Light Infantry. I was billeted at Sontley Camp on the racecourse. After a few days getting sorted out, sending our civil clothes homes and getting our uniforms etc, we were drafted to A Company, which was made up of four squads - A, B, C and D.

'The first few weeks were hard work - training, route marches, physical training and guarding. The route marches were stiff. We started with three miles and increased it up to 12 miles. Sometimes the band would come and meet us and play us back to camp. We spent some time on the rifle range before getting our provisionary pay and passing out.

'After some time, we were being posted to Hastings for more training - out on schemes under live fire. There were tapes down in certain areas which signified land mine areas, which we had to avoid.

'After a time, we moved on again to a place in Sussex called Ferring-on-Sea, which was on the sea front. Our duties involved guarding the Block Houses. We had a bren gun on a tripod, which was set to a certain degree to match up with all the others on the beach. At night, when on duty, we would have to take the rations down to the troops on guard. We had to be careful as the path was taped off to help us avoid the land mines. We also worked at the Little Hampton Hospital, guarding German soldiers who had been shot down. We then moved further on to the coast of the Irish Sea for more training, as it was said that the Germans were planning an invasion. Whether it was true or not we did not know.

'From there, we moved again to Invarary in Scotland, where we began invasion training. We had to climb down from the side of a ship with full equipment down a scrambling net. 'Then we had to leave our equipment, in case we fell into the water, and make our way as quickly as possible onto landing craft and assault boats.

'This went on for several weeks before we were moved again to Selkirk, stationed at a place call the Hainings.

'At this time, I was appointed Batman to Captain J W Simmons, who was the Weapons Training Officer - spending my time in the officers' mess at the County Hotel. I was able to get my wife Marion up for a few weeks and had a sleeping out pass. While we were at Selkirk, we practised gas raids while wearing our gas masks.

'One morning, Captain Simmons told me to tell my wife I was going on a weekend scheme with the First Battalion Commandos. We arrived at Harwich, and the following day, lined the streets as Winston Churchill was coming to inspect us. We had been there some time when a car carrying him drove past. This was all we saw of him before we boarded a ship that would carry us to war.

'There was no way I could let Marion know where I was going, as all our mail was censored - it would be six months before she would find out where I was. We had been out to sea for about a week when we found out where we were going. Captain Simmons told us it was South Africa. We were on the water, in convoy with other ships, for about six weeks when we arrived at Durban.

'During our short stay there, we underwent more invasion training at Mobassa in East Africa and in Zulu land, where we visited the area where the Boar War was fought, and a church together with the graves of the soldiers buried there.

'We then set off to the Indian Ocean, and it was then I found out we were going to invade Madagascar, as it was rumoured the Japanese were coming.

'On the morning of May 5, we were told we would land at 5.30am, and everybody was given a tot of ship's rum. Then we got into the ALC boats and set off. While on the water, we were fired on by our Allies, as they must have thought we were the invading Japanese. We eventually landed on the beach, and after some time getting assembled, we began to make our way. We had been moving a few hours when we were told to stop and take our rations, which consisted of a small tin of corned beef, some biscuits, a water warmer for our tea and a small pot of jam. We had to put our biscuits in a mess tin of water to soften them. When we had finished, we were putting back what rations were left into our rucksacks when we discovered they were already full - of red ants! So that was that.

'We then set off for the capital - Diego Squarries, and arrived without any trouble. We did two more landings - at Tamataire and Tenereive. We stayed in Madagascar for about five months and then got back onto the ships after being told we were on our way home. However, the brigade got word that the First Indian Division were pinned down by the Japanese, so we moved on to India and landed at Bombay.

'From there, we were transported to Poona where we did more training and guarding. It was in Poona that I saw Mahatma Gandhi. I also managed to go to the Taj Mahal to see my brother-in-law, who was recovering in hospital there. While in India, we had to make sure we took quinine and put nets up over our beds because of the mosquitoes. We were also able to visit the Lady Lumley's canteen. She was a very nice person.

'It was soon time to move again, as we first went to Calcutta before sailing to Chittagong. We landed under covering fire in the early morning and made our way up the beach as quickly as possible to look for cover. It was very difficult, as we hadn't been trained for jungle warfare.

'Later, we managed to get to the Aracan, where we stayed for a while. At one stage, we had to cross the Irrawaddy River. It was only about 20 yards wide at our crossing point, but we still had to send our best swimmers across

first with toddle ropes. We had to hold onto the rope and pull ourselves across. The water was calm on the surface, but with very strong undercurrents that could easily pull you under. Several bush hats floated down it!

'We had been in Aracan for some time when we were told of a special visitor coming to

talk to the brigade - it proved to be Lord Mountbatten. He had a meal with us, he ate out of a mess tin as we did, and then slept rough with us. When his stay came to an end, he gathered us all together and told us that even though he was the king's cousin, we were not to worry. He was no different to us. He said we were all there to do a job, and the sooner that job was done, the sooner we could all go home. Also, he would not have anyone do anything he could not do himself.

'After a week or two, we had to learn to fly wooden gliders to enable us to land at a place called Shebab, where a sugar factory had been overtaken by the Japanese. We landed the gliders and soon had control of the factory. We found out from the Medical Officer stationed in the factory that the Japanese had mistreated a family living there. They had been raped. The husband of this family asked if he could join us, as he knew the country. He soon became our guide.

'As we made our way towards the capital, we had all sorts of setbacks. Mosquitoes, snakes, scorpions and leeches to name a few! When we entered swamp water, we had to burn the leeches using lit cigarettes. When we were camped, and guarding the perimeter, the Japanese, who knew who they were up against, would shout 'Hello Taffy' in English. They were very clever soldiers. They made good use of camouflage. When we were out on patrol, they would let the first section pass and then capture the others.

'We carried on fighting through the monsoons, and it was when guarding a perimeter that I lost my earplugs along with the others, and ended up going to hospital with a busted eardrum. I was transferred to the field hospital, and from there, to a hospital in Boolate.

'The first thing I got was a jab for bubonic plague.

During this time, the war in England was said to be over. We celebrated with the officers there and put on a party for them.

'A short time after, the war was declared over in Burma, so the officers returned the compliment and waited on us for the day! Then I was due for de-mob. I moved with others onto a ship.

I arrived in England just before Christmas 1945 and managed to get home the week before Christmas Day.

I went back to Ashton-Under-Lyne for de-mob and then back home to my wife and family in the first week of January 1946.

'I am glad to say Captain Simmons was awarded the Military Cross for Madagascar. We should be proud of Wingale and his Chindits - some of the single men from our brigade had to go with him.

They were dropped behind enemy lines. Some of the lads never returned due to malaria and other diseases. They were under the most difficult conditions. We remember General Wingale dying on the way home.

God bless them all."

POWs welcome their liberators

A tale of brutality, starvation and death...

"Horror march that reduced scores of tough fighting men into physical wrecks"

Words by Terry Morgan

Taken from the Bury Times, April 18, 1945 Two Bury Men Were On Prisoners' Horror March. "One a day died," says soldier. Both liberated from the same prison camp by the Americans, but unknown to each other, two local men have arrived home to tell their stories of the death marches across Germany. One, a Glider Pilot blinded before he was captured at Arnhem, trekked with the airborne heroes in a horror march that reduced scores of these tough fighting men into physical wrecks. The other, a RASC Driver in captivity since Crete in June 1941, was among British prisoners marched more than 500 miles through raging blizzards until men died of frostbite and exhaustion.

The two men are Staff Sergeant Peter Louchrin Martin of Hollins Lane, Unsworth, and Driver John Francis Wilson of Fenton Street, Bury.

Their hardships ended on Good Friday of this year, when American tanks crashed through to the camp where they were held between Kassel and Frankfurt.

Driver Wilson (then aged 28), tells in his own words how he managed to survive the seven weeks of almost unbelievable privations.

"I was in a working party employed at Breslau gas works and attached to Stalag 8C on the Polish border. We knew about the Russian advance from our secret radio, and when the Russians were only 25km away, we were told to pack our kit and be ready to march on January 24. They told us we would only be marching for three days, but that was all bluff.

We were tramping continuously from January 24 to the middle of March.

'At the start, we were given a Red Cross parcel containing one-and-a-half weeks' issue of food for each man, and when that ran out, all they gave us was a 2kg loaf between four men and 50g of margarine for two men each day. Sometimes, if we were lucky, we got a cup of ersatz coffee made from burnt wheat.

'Blizzards were raging when we began the march and we had to sleep in our saturated clothing at night in barns or under any shelter we could find. We had no hot foot and no facilities for heating it, had there been any during the whole of the journey.

'When we came to open the tins of bully beef in our Red Cross parcels, we found they were frozen and so had to eat them like that.

The Germans brought our bread ration on horse-drawn carts, covered only with a sheet of calico, and when they gave it to us, it was sodden.

'The Germans gave us no water and we had to eat melted snow to quench our thirst. Then, they only began to dish out our rations intermittently and the men we so hungry they began pulling up swedes and other root crops and eating them raw. There was a great deal of dysentery and frostbite, but the prisoners were made to march in spite of this. Deaths averaged one a day.

'The Jerries gave us no transport whatsoever for our sick, and I have seen with my own eyes a fellow with his feet swollen to three times the normal size and black from frostbite. He was still made to march, and when the interpreter pleaded for transport for him, the German Commandant in charge of the party told the guard to make sure that this man was kept marching. When he marched slowly, he was struck by the guard with his rifle.

'Quite a number of men were marching barefoot through the snow, with their feet bound in rags. I myself had two pairs of boots when I started out, and these fortunately lasted me the whole of the march. My feet were blistered and I had dysentery but I did not suffer so much as many of the men.

'Once, we went entirely without food for four days, and when we felt we could stand it no longer, we told the Commandant that we would march no further without rations. He threatened to bring out the machine gun battalion and forced us to continue, but when we all still refused to march, he eventually told us that if we continued for another 15 kilometres, we would be given a hot meal. We started off again but when we reached our destination, a farm, we found that the 'hot meal' consisted of one-and-a-half potatoes per man and cup of coffee.

'Many German civilians were hostile to us, but some of them gave us bread and I have seen instances where the guards beat women with their rifle-butts for giving food to the prisoners. You could see from the faces of the civilians that they were war-weary, and if you got a chance to speak to them, they told you they were absolutely fed up with the war.

'We were all ill after more than 40 days' marching and starvation, but the Commandant of the camp now ordered us to dig air raid shelters for the officers and staff of the camp. Our MOs protested that we were in no state to do this after a 500-mile march and Red Cross officials visited the camp and appealed to the Germans on our behalf, but all protests were ignored and we were set to work at the digging. Four or five men died from exhaustion from this. 'The Frenchmen, who had their own secret radio, told us about the British and American advances in our direction and the Jerries seemed to realise the position was getting pretty hopeless. The digging stopped, they gave us better soup and promised us more rations in future to build the men up again."

A similar tale of brutality, starvation and death came from the then 24-year-old Staff Sergeant Martin, captured with other British wounded from Arnhem Hospital, where he lay blinded for three days after being wounded in the battle. "The Jerries were afraid of the airborne troops/ They called us 'gangsters' and they would not even let us get out for water on the journey when they took us by cattle truck to Westphalia," he said.

When the Arnhem captives went in through the prison gates whistling tunes, the German Commandant threatened to shoot them "if their aggressive attitude did not alter."

At a transit camp, their watches and other valuables were taken from them.

"Later, we were sent to a camp in Silesia, again in cattle trucks. Throughout the holes which we carved in the sides of the trucks, we saw one of the greatest sights of our stay in Germany -

Berlin completely flattened by air raids as we passed through.

'On the morning of February 7, eight to 10,000 of us, including French, Russians and Serbs, left the camp at Sagan where we had been taken. Everything was absolutely disorganised and the Germans just marched us and marched us without food and without aim. For three successive nights, in intense cold, we slept in the open on football pitches."

On one occasion, the starving prisoners ate burnt bread which they found in a bakery that had been destroyed by fire. On the 19th day, men were dropping by the roadside with exhaustion and Staff Sergeant Martin became too ill to go any further. Eventually, 85 of the more sick prisoners, including himself, were packed into an open cattle truck and travelled in it for 26 hours - too tightly packed to move. 'Rations' for the journey consisted of one loaf between 12 men and a tin of bully beef between 14.

"We had been on the road for 44 days when we reached Stalag 9A, and all were in a very bad state. The following morning, we awoke to find that four of our chaps had died. 'We heard the news of the American advance on the concealed radio, and when everyone started cheering, the Germans searched repeatedly for it but couldn't find it.

'On the Thursday morning, the Germans moved 5,000 prisoners out and left about 3,000 of us in the camp hospital. It was just a matter of suspense from then on. On Friday morning, from the camp hospital we saw the first tanks and vehicles move past and we recognised them as American from their white star. Then, when a jeep came and stopped at the camp about four in the afternoon, the prisoners just broke down the wire and rushed out to the greet the driver and hoist him shoulder-high. Men were hobbling out on sticks and some literally crawling - they all wanted to be there to see the great sight."

Prisoners marched without food or water for days on end

Local heroes: A report from the Bury Times, March 31, 1945

Words by Terry Morgan

GEORGE MEDAL

Former leading personality in local amateur dramatics, and Gunner in the Royal Artillery, Harry Barnes of Walmersley Road, Bury, has been awarded the George Medal for gallantry.

He lost a leg in Holland when he trod on an anti-personnel mine in going to the assistance of a comrade whose foot had been blown off.

The official citation records: "On November 25, 1944, the regimental reconnaissance party was ordered to reconnoitre and survey gun positions some miles west of Venlo, an area known to be mined. One member of the survey party accidentally walked some distance into a minefield, where his foot was blown off by an anti-personnel mine.

'Gunner Barnes entered the minefield, and as he reached the injured man, he trod on another mine, his leg being blown off at the knee. In spite of this, he dragged himself to safety, urging and encouraging the other man to follow him. Throughout, he remained clear-headed, doing what he could to assist his comrade, whose life in all probability he saved."

DISTINGUISHED FLYING MEDAL

Home on leave last weekend, Pilot Officer George Collins Heywood of Leyland Street, Bury, did not tell his parents that he had won the Distinguished Flying Medal.

His mother had a surprise when a Bury Times reporter brought her news this week that her son had won the medal for "numerous operations in which the utmost fortitude, courage and devotion to duty was displayed."

Pilot Officer Heywood, who is 30, has completed 30 operational flights and has been in the Air Force for more than three years.

Recently, with six other members of the crew, he was rescued after several hours in a dingy when the Lancaster he was flying as navigator caught fire and crashed into the sea.

He was a member of Bury Sports Club and previously played in the hockey and football teams at high school.

Before joining the RAF, he was a member of the Air Training Corps at Bury and worked as a costing clerk at the Bury Felt manufacturing company.

His father, Arthur Heywood, former musical director of Bury Hippodrome, is now working for the Air Ministry.

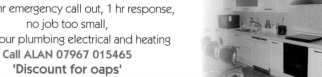

Vital role behind the scenes...

"New Year's Eve, thank God - are we winning the war?"

Words by Terry Morgan

Richard McLoughlin never spoke a great deal about his experiences during the war, but the carefully kept diaries, letters and photos documenting the years were indications that it was not something he wanted to erase from his, or future generations' memories.

His daughter, Sue Bell, explained how despite his reticence about what he experienced, it was extremely important to her father that people remember what was sacrificed.

Sadly, Mr McLoughlin passed away eight years ago, but his family continue to honour his memory and service to the country. Sue's son, Robert Bibby, goes to the Cenotaph every Remembrance Sunday to commemorate the fallen, as he promised his grandfather before he died.

Private McLoughlin joined the 8th Army Catering Corps when he was 19, and was to spend the next five years abroad - travelling extensively as the 8th Army 'Desert Rats' fought all over North Africa, the Middle East and Italy - then in Austria and Greece towards and after the end of the war.

His carefully kept notes list the names of the places he visited: Tripoli, Sorrento, Rome, Jerusalem, Beirut, Cairo, Baghdad, Vienna, Graz, Athens.

A baker and confectioner by trade, Mr McLoughlin left his job at Royle's Bakery in Radcliffe and worked as a cook for the 8th Army. It is often the soldiers that were involved in the actual fighting that are thought of first when it comes to wartime remembrance, but those behind the scenes, such as the Catering Corps, played a vital role.

"Many people think that only those who were fighting on the front line saw the horrors of war," said Sue, "but the Catering Corps were right behind those soldiers, so my dad was also witness to some awful sights."

The diaries that contain most detail of life during the war are from 1944, when the 8th Army went to fight the Axis in Italy. The entries are short and stoic, yet descriptive. The first one, on December 31, 1943, is an indication of how the soldiers lived in their own sphere - not knowing what was actually going on in the rest of the war.

"I am going to bed. What's the use of staying up in the cold, we have not got a drink to celebrate. New Year's Eve, thank God - are we winning the war?"

January 6: "Well today I left for up the front (in Naples). I think I am going to like this job, but there was plenty of shelling from the other side today, and plenty of planes in the sky."

The following weeks show days of continuous shelling of the village where the unit was camped, documenting plenty of close shaves.

January 28: "I was very lucky today as a shell fell 10 yards away from the cookhouse - thought I'd had it."

The soldiers rarely knew where they were headed or when they would be granted leave, getting information more or less on a daily basis. Looking into the future was not something that was encouraged.

March 11: "Today we moved into camp for a night before we go on the boat. There's talk of going home. God I hope so."

Unfortunately, Mr McLoughlin's hopes were not met, but the men were granted leave within Italy, during which they did their best to enjoy themselves and forget the war around them.

June 6: "It's (the invasion) started now, I wonder if it will last a year - still it's nice to know that we are back once again. Good luck to the lads."

As well as the shelling and conflict, daily life in Army camp had its own risks and tragedies.

September 14: "We had an accident today. Two of the lads got shot trough the neck by a fellow cleaning his gun. One has died, poor lad."

The fighting in Italy intensified in the latter part of 1944, and the diary entries become more morbid.

September 22, 1944: "I took a walk out this afternoon and got a shock. In a cave on a hill, I found four dead people - must have been dead for ages - three men and a girl and not a stitch of clothing on. Half an hour later, the Italians came along and poured petrol on them, as they did not half smell, and set light. I took my hook, couldn't stand it."

September 26, 1944: "The village on top of the hill smells of dead. It's believed that hundreds of people were killed through shelling."

This is the last entry in the diary, and is a haunting reminder of the effects of war. Much of what he saw, Mr McLoughlin kept to himself, not wanting to speak of the atrocities. But his daughter remembers that one thing her father had often mentioned was the kindness of

Richard McLoughlin wanted people to acknowledge and remember the sacrifice of others

civilians in Italy, particularly the Catholic priests in the small villages the soldiers camped in.

"He always spoke highly of them, as many did not agree with their own Government and the Nazi occupation and would help the Allied soldiers, telling them the right direction when the signs had been hidden or destroyed and giving them food.

'Several times, the priests hid my father and other soldiers in wine barrels in the cellar until the Italians or Germans had left the area."

Mr McLoughlin became a master baker at Royle's.

On the surface, life was very similar to the one he had left in 1939, but what he had been through during the war meant that underneath, life would never be the same again.

THE NATION'S BIGGEST THANK YOU
FOR VICTORY IN 1945

WWII ANNIVERSARY APPEAL BY THE ROYAL BRITISH LEGION

To mark the 60th anniversary of the end of the Second World War, The Royal British Legion is launching a national campaign to say a 'Big Thank You' to all those men and women who fought for our freedom 60 years ago.

The aim of 'The Nation's Biggest Thank You' is to give each of us the opportunity to express our gratitude to everyone who played a part in Britain's heroic war effort. It may well be our last opportunity to do this as a nation.

This campaign is not about singling out individual heroes - it's about acknowledging the heroism of every single man and woman who took part - Churchill's 'Unknown Warriors.'

Whether in the jungle in Burma, on the beaches of Normandy or in a munitions factory in Manchester, everyone was indispensable to the success of the war effort and every single person deserves our wholehearted gratitude and respect.

To sum up the aspirations of the campaign, The British Legion has designed a 'Victory Thanks' logo which will feature throughout the campaign.

It is an attempt to symbolise the enormous significance of this anniversary and to convey the nation's immense gratitude, pride and respect for the men and women whose suffering and sacrifice made possible the freedom we enjoy today.

For more information about the campaign, visit www.victorythanks.org.uk

Help The British Legion to say 'Thanks for Victory'

In order to make this campaign a success, The British Legion needs your help. Here are just a few ways that you can get involved in helping the Legion say a big thank you for the freedom we enjoy today:

Throw a 'Victory Thanks Party'

Inspired by the street parties which happened spontaneously all over the country as Victory in Europe was announced on May 8 1945, the Legion has put together a party pack which contains everything you need to hold your own 'Victory Thanks Party.'

It includes posters, bunting, banners, balloons, badges and stickers plus a booklet on how to run your own successful party.

The Legion has also included an A-Z of fundraising ideas so that you can help support their welfare work at the same time.

To order your pack, telephone 01622 795815

or visit www.victorythanks.org.uk

Wear a badge to show your support

The public will be able to show their support for the campaign by wearing a Victory Thanks lapel badge, which will be available at many major retailers and pub chains.

There is a suggested donation of £2 for each badge.

Write a message of thanks

You can also show your gratitude to all Second World War veterans by writing a message of thanks on the back of a Victory Thanks bunting flag and sending this back to The British Legion with a donation.

Each of these individual messages of thanks will be made up into lengths of bunting and displayed in Trafalgar Square on July 10 - End of WWII Day - forming a dramatic and poignant culmination to The Nation's Biggest Thank You campaign.

If you would like to write a message to say 'Thanks for Victory,' please telephone 0845 8451945 or visit the website www.victorythanks.org.uk

FEARLESS

60 years ago, George was hunting U-Boats.
Today we help keep his head above water.

The North Atlantic, 1943. Heroes are needed. An elite unit is formed to take on the Nazi U-Boats who are destroying allied merchant ships with impunity.

Able Seaman George Enoch Atkins is one of those heroes. It's dangerous work, it's deadly work. Through luck, skill and sheer bravery, George lives through it when many of his comrades do not.

Yet his hardest battle lies ahead. These days, age and illness have taken their toll on George. He needed help and we are proud and honoured to give it.

We are here for all the other ex-Servicemen and women and their families, too.

From survivors of the World Wars through to those who served in more recent troubles in Bosnia and The Gulf and on to the many thousands serving around the world who may need us one day.

People like George did their duty. We will never forsake ours. Now or in the future.

THE NATION'S BIGGEST THANK YOU FOR VICTORY IN 1945
WWII ANNIVERSARY APPEAL BY THE ROYAL BRITISH LEGION

THE ROYAL BRITISH LEGION

The Royal British Legion. Always on active service. **www.britishlegion.org.uk** 08457 725 725

There is nothing heroic about war...

"I was still in Rangoon on August 14, 1945, and at first, we had no idea the Japanese had surrendered"

Words by Karen Openshaw

Former Mayor of Bury, Winston Ramsey, may have been in the 'Forgotten Army' serving in Burma, but his memories of the end of the Second World War remain as vivid as ever.

"I was still in Rangoon on August 14, 1945, and at first, we had no idea the Japanese had surrendered," he recalled.

"The problem was that communication was terribly difficult, so no one was quite sure what the situation was."

The news was made official later in the day, but the beleaguered Mr Ramsey and his comrades did not celebrate.

"I can't remember any elation. An Italian band did play for us, and we were promised a bottle of beer, but we never got it. We all knew we had a job to do and after the relief of it all, we just wanted to get home as soon as possible.

'It was the same with VE Day. We were obviously pleased that the war was over but all it meant to us was that we might have a chance of having better supplies sent to us."

Mr Ramsey, aged 75 of Victor Avenue, joined the Army a month after the war began at the tender age of 20 and spent six-and-a-half years serving King and Country. A full Sergeant in the Royal Engineers, he went to Burma in 1944 after training in Northern India.

He said: "Lord Mountbatten told us plainly that it was up to us to stop the Japanese. We had a job to do and that is what we did. There is nothing heroic about war. It was disease and suffering. I had malaria and jungle sores and although I weighed almost 11 stones when I joined up, I was just seven stones eight when I left."

Mr Ramsey, one of Bury's longest-serving councillors, will be remembering his fallen comrades when he attends the VJ Service in London on Sunday.

Winston Ramsey

Our war was part of a secret history that nobody talks about...

"I am returning to pay my respects to the people of Vietnam"

Words by Terry Morgan

Radcliffe pensioner Phil Kaiserman has been given the chance to make an emotional return to Vietnam - 60 years after he served there during the Second World War.

In August, Phil will travel to Saigon under the Big Lottery Fund's Heroes Return, but it will be a journey of mixed feelings.

"I am returning to pay my respects to the people of Vietnam," he explained, "because of what I was involved in there during the Second World War."

Mr Kaiserman's commitment to former French Indochina and its people is not in doubt.

Over the years, he has helped raise more than £1 million to build a hospital there and he is a veteran of the Peace in Vietnam campaign; as well as an active voluntary archivist of labour movement material about the country.

He said: "I was posted to Saigon in 1945 after travelling across India with RAF Commando Unit 3209. Our war was part of a secret history that nobody talks much about. In effect, I believe we were helping the occupying French forces to suppress the local population and ensure that Vietnam would remain a French colony."

Under the Potsdam Agreement of 1945 between the Allied powers, British forces were to control southern Vietnam - which had been occupied by the Japanese and ruled through most of the war by the Vichy French administration.

Britain handed power in southern Vietnam back to the French, then under the de Gaulle Government, who briefly recognised Ho Chi Minh's Vietminh administration in north Vietnam.

Mr Kaiserman, of Grosvenor Street, Radcliffe, said: "My strongest recollection of my service in Vietnam is of looking into the window of a Saigon jail and seeing a Vietnamese prisoner suspended from a hook in the ceiling being brutally beaten and tortured by the French. I will carry the memory to my grave."

After he was demobbed in 1947, Mr Kaiserman returned to the Salford area and his old trade as a barber.

He and his wife Clare bought their first home in Russell Street, Prestwich, and in 1984, the couple moved to their current home and Mr Kaiserman started working at Radcliffe Paper Mill.

When he retired, the father of two became involved in pensioners' rights and was a founder member of Bury Pensioners Association.

Phil Kaiserman today

A secret love that blossomed in spite of the war that raged around it

"I was a Sergeant and she was an Officer!"

Albert Winstanley during the war
Below: Kathleen in 1944

Words by Frank Elson

Albert Winstanley had a secret while he was in North Africa, serving in the biggest military hospital of that campaign- he fell in love with a nurse. "We had to keep it a secret," remembers Albert, "I was a Sergeant and she was an Officer!"

Love blossomed in the heat of a fierce campaign and Albert and his nurse were married in Bolton after the war. Operation Torch, the Allied invasion of Morocco and Algeria, is something of an oddity in the history of the Second World War. The Americans fought the French; the invasion (often said to have been the rehearsal for Normandy) was actually on Vichy French sovereign soil. The French Governor, installed after an agreement with Eisenhower, was thought by many to have been a Nazi collaborator and was quickly assassinated; and many historians believe that Rommel was already beaten by that time. Of course, to a young Sergeant in the Medical Corps, none of that mattered. In mid-November 1942, three-and-a-half weeks after leaving Sussex, Albert Winstanley landed on a beach in Algeria and began setting up a hospital in a town called Benni Mesous. Albert stayed at the hospital during and after the invasion of Italy. One of the nurses who took part in the landings in Sicily and Italy was struck down by malaria while in Italy. As fate would have it, she was shipped back to Albert's hospital.

"What can I say? We fell in love," says Albert. "But we had to keep it a secret. She outranked me!" The couple married after the war and were together until Kathleen died in 1997.

Among other more mundane duties, Albert was in charge of burials. "Being called to go and collect the tags from all these dead young men, often picking up arms and legs and matching them to the rest of the body, ascertaining if their death was natural or through act of war; it had to be done," says Albert.

"Then I had to record all the details loved ones needed to know and, even in the middle of a campaign, war pensions had to be thought of. Then I arranged the funeral. At first, we buried them wrapped in a blanket, but the Arabs used to dig them up to steal the blankets. That stopped when I got the engineers to make us some wooden coffins.

The Arabs didn't seem to want wood. I joined up in 1939. I wanted to go. It sounds a bit trite now, but I wanted to do my bit," says the 87-year-old.

Albert and Kathleen enjoyed a long and happy marriage

That's how it happened – some lived and some died...

"He was my best mate and I'll never forget him"

Words by Frank Elson

The difference between being alive today and being able to pass on some memories of the Second World War and not making it back often depended on so little. Take the story of Bolton's Albert Tyrer and Jack Cronshaw, from Darwen. In 1940, there was a shortage of signallers in the Middle East. As a result, Albert and Jack were transferred from the Bolton Artillery Regiment to the 97th Field Regiment of the Kent Yeomanry and sent to Almazo camp on the outskirts of Cairo.

The two friends were linesmen and they got a little extra pay as 'tradesmen,' their job being to lay out the signal lines between artillery batteries and OPs (Observation Posts) and to maintain them, repairing breaks in the wires. This job was not without its dangers, for OPs were, of necessity, in view of the enemy so that officers could let the artillery know where their shells were landing.

The pair served throughout the Western Desert campaign, including the eventual capture of Tobruk, and with the rest of the Eighth Army landed in Italy.

At one time, volunteers were called for to lay a line to an OP behind enemy lines. Jack volunteered and set off with a gunnery sergeant, an OP Officer and a platoon of Indian infantry.

Before too long, the patrol was ambushed and met a hail of gunfire.

The Indian Officer was killed and the OP Officer took command.

He soon decided that the patrol was a failure and ordered the withdrawal back to Allied lines.

On the way back Jack, known as JC to his friends, stepped on a mine which blew off his foot. Despite being partially blinded by the same explosion, the Gunnery Sergeant carried Jack for miles until he was completely exhausted.

Jack was then able to persuade the others to leave him with some cigarettes and matches and send a well-armed patrol out for him later on. However, two days later, Jack was found by a patrol with three German stretcher-bearers. All dead, killed by a British artillery barrage... Today, Albert Tyrer is 84 years old and well aware that it could have just as easily been him

as Jack. "It was the war. He was my best mate for a time and I'll never forget him, but that's how it happened, some lived and some died," said Albert. "I had a dog called Dizzy. One morning, we were out checking a line and his fur stood on end and he growled. I peered over a gully edge and there were two Germans following the line. I took them prisoner."

Albert Tyrer today

For the sake of the Jews...

Bill Grime today

"I did get my hair parted by a bullet one time. That was as close as I wanted to get"

Words by Frank Elson

Bill Grime should not have been in the Army, let alone in North Africa. Bill was the original nine-stone weakling and not in good health when his call-up papers arrived. However, as he put it himself: "I managed to get in and after that, the Army helped to get me fit." He then added, with a twinkle in his eye: "Mind you, they then proceeded to try to get me killed a few times!"

As a signaller in the Leicester Yeomanry, Bill was on the front line at El Alamein and frequently slightly in front of the line.

He will never forget the opening barrage in which, as an Artillery Signaller, he played an important part. "It was the most fantastic sight and sound you could imagine," he said.

"One of our batteries fired 600 rounds in the first day. Of course, then Jerry was after us because the guns were useless without us. Keeping your head down was a very good idea! I did get my hair parted by a bullet one time. That was as close as I wanted to get."

Bill, from Bolton, shouldn't even have been in North Africa. "We were actually on our way to India when Monty decided he wanted more guns and where they went, we went."

Being shot at was one thing, but that wasn't all bothering Bill and his mates. "We were all suffering from 'gyppy tummy,' which is not pleasant at the best of times. And being in a hole trying to tell guns what to aim at is certainly not the best of times!

'I remember one night, when I was still ill, we were being shot at and the telephone wire went down. When that happened, someone had to crawl from each end of the wire looking for the break. So I set off on my hands and knees from our end. I crawled for a half a mile until I got to HQ to find that the wire had just pulled out at their end and none of them had gone out to sort it. I said a few things that you can't tell your readers!" For all his other problems, the young Bill Grime was blessed with good eyesight, something that came in particularly useful in the early stages of the battle.

"It was quite difficult to tell the difference between a Fokker Wolfe 109 and a Hurricane (fighter planes) when they came zipping along, close to the ground. That is, until they shot at us. But I could tell the difference, so when one appeared, all my mates looked at me to find out whether to hit the deck or not. 'Mind you, visibility wasn't a lot better for the pilots so we ended up hitting the deck whoever it was because both sides would shoot sometimes."

Bill and his gunners moved a few times during the main battle, fighting first with a group of Free French from Central Africa- "some of the best fighters I have ever met,"- before going into action in support of an Indian Regiment which consisted mainly of Gurkhas- "definitely the best fighters I have ever met!"

Bill has been a supporter of the Gurkha Welfare Trust since the war as a result of those few weeks spent with the men from Nepal.

In the last few days of the battle of El Alamein, when mopping up and mobility were the mainstays, heavy guns were not needed. Almost before the battle had ended, Bill and his comrades who had survived were pulled out of the line. "We were actually headed for Stalingrad after that. Can you believe the Army? They were now trying to get me killed from cold instead of heat!"

However, a plan which saw Bill and his pals travel through Palestine, Iraq and Iran on their way to Stalingrad actually came to nothing when the war ended the following year.

So why did Bill "fool" the medical examiner? Why was he so desperate to go to war in the first place?

"I went to fight mainly because it was leaking out what the Germans were doing to the Jews," he said. "Hitler wasn't going to stop. He was evil."

I spent the next six years not knowing anything other than war...

"This party for you, children, is to commemorate World Peace, which was declared on August 15th, 1945, after nearly six years of war"

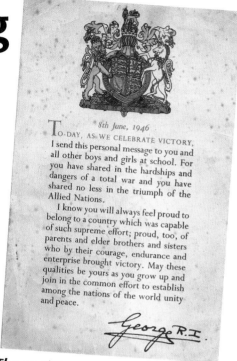

The certificate signed by King George VI and handed out to schoolchildren around the country

Words by Frank Elson

Born in 1939, Edward Higson spent the next six years not knowing anything other than war. "It was simply the normal way of living, I knew nothing else," said Mr Higson of Deane, Bolton.

"For instance, my mother had a Mrs Beaton Cookery Book. In it were pictures of butchers' shops with meat hanging up all around. I didn't believe the book because I knew what a butcher's shop looked like- an empty window and nothing hanging up. I asked my mother why the pictures were wrong and she said it was because of the war, but I don't really think she explained what war was. 'Rationing was just a fact of life. Again I knew nothing else, and when I started school in 1944, all the families were one-parent; all the men were away.

'Again, this seemed perfectly natural to me. My father worked on the railways and died in 1944 but I didn't feel any different to anyone else because their fathers weren't around either. I remember tanks from the Beaumont Road maintenance unit parked in four rows from Wigan Road to Chorley New Road. There was a hut for the people who worked there and we used to go to scrounge sweets and chocolate off them and there were barrage balloons in the

sky, but then I don't remember them not being there! 'Grown-ups didn't try to keep the war a secret, but they just didn't discuss it with children of my age. We had a food parcel once from America, maybe my mother got it because she was a widow, but I remember a huge block of Rockwood's chocolate was in it. It had ridges across it, not squares.

'When the war ended, I don't remember any special celebrations either. The headmaster at Deane Primary handed out the certificate signed by the King (pictured) almost a year later and, going to my grandmother's, house all the houses had "welcome home" banners outside but that would have been well after the war finished of course.

'My most vivid memory of that period was being taken to the top of Quebec Street at night to watch Bolton's gas streetlights being turned on again. The time had been announced and there was quite a crowd. There were not as many houses blocking the view as there are today and it was quite spectacular. I was completely amazed. I had grown up in the dark and simply did not realise that street lighting was possible! I can't remember what I thought lamp posts were for, they were just there."

Born in 1942, Mr Higson's wife Eva remembers even less of the war, but she was

able to show us an interesting item of memorabilia in the form of the leaflet (pictured) for 'A Grand Party' for children organised by the residents of Carter Street, Sadler Street, Bradford Road and Crescent Road in August 1945.

"I really don't remember the war, or the party," said Mrs Higson, "but my father, Frank Bain, wrote the message inside."

The leaflet described a full programme of sports events, pony rides (on 'Peggy') and entertainment by both children and adults, plus a potato pie supper.

The message, written by Mrs Higson's father, reads:

"This party for you, children, is to commemorate World Peace, which was declared on August 15th, 1945, after nearly six years of war. Perhaps you may, or may not, remember the hardship and sorrow created by this war, for as much of it as possible has been kept away from you by your parents, and it is hoped that you will keep this Souvenir Programme as long as you live, in order that you may look at it sometimes, and remember the happy time you had after so much sorrow. It is the hope of every parent that never in your life will you have to go through such a war as the one that has just ended."

Bombing the Bridge on the River Kwai

Ernest Marsden (far left) with the rest of his crew

"We had to fly under monsoon clouds as well, because they could rip the wings off the plane"

Words by Frank Elson

Bombing the bridge on the River Kwai was just another job for Ernest Marsden. The retired Bolton schoolteacher, a navigator in Bomber Command South East Asia, only found out its importance after the war.

"There were two bridges, a wooden one and a steel and concrete one, and these were the only ways over the river. The Japs moved men and materials across them and they had to come down. We were aware that they were being worked on by Prisoners of War but the bridges had to come down. It was our job.

'I was with 159 Squadron and we went over there with another squadron and put the bridge down." As a navigator with none of the modern navigational aids, Ernest had to work out the plane's position by dead reckoning.

Today, he is justifiably proud of finding the bridge after covering around 1,000 miles from the base in India. "To get there, drop our bombs and then find our way back after a 2,000 mile round trip was some effort yes, I'm proud of it. I was never scared on the trips, most of which were out over the water of the Bay of Bombay. I was too busy. I had to work out our position every 15 minutes or so."

Out of 23 raids that Ernest took part in after arriving in India in 1944, the one that he is most proud of resulted in the destruction of an oil tanker out to sea.

"We were told to find this convoy. We did it, got the tanker and returned after a round trip of 2,600 miles. The skipper (pilot) got the DFC for that, the rest of us got SFA (Sweet Fanny Adams- RAF slang for nothing)!"

Ernest went from Bolton to Canada after volunteering for the RAF on his 18th birthday in 1942.

"I wanted to be a navigator and volunteering was the way to get the job you wanted. In Canada, I wanted to go into Transport Command, was sent to this place and found I was in Bomber Command! The Liberator bomber that we flew had a crew of 11 and we all trained together. We then went to India where I had to join another crew who had lost their navigator through illness. So all that training together was a waste of time.

'The new bomb aimer was useless compared to the man I trained with. One day, we had to drop mines in a river mouth. You cannot drop them from too high or they will explode on impact, so we were flying up this river very low with ack ack either side of us. He had to find this island and then start dropping the mines. Could he find it? Could he heck! He did eventually of course, but that was a very hairy time." Supply runs were also "interesting" in Ernest's mind.

"We had to fly very low, 'tree height' they called it, and more than once we found bits of foliage in our landing gear when we got back. And we had to fly under monsoon clouds as well, because they could rip the wings off a plane. This meant around 400 feet, which over the sea is not amusing!"

Having arrived in India in late 1944, bombing raids soon petered out when the war ended, but Ernest and his crew stayed on for another few years dropping food and aid to refugees and displaced persons.

"We went all over South East Asia, even as far as Vietnam one time. We weren't being shot at but hanging inside a plane pushing rice sacks out with your feet was worrying enough!"

Today, the 80-year-old great grandfather is, like many veterans, surprised and slightly upset by the way they are looked at by younger people. "I wasn't a hero; I don't want adulation, but a lot of people died in that war all those years ago to preserve the freedoms that today are taken for granted. I don't think it's wrong to want to remember that."

Keeping the home fires burning: Our last line of defence

The Home Front

Words by Alan Domville

Long before the Government had accepted the possibility of war with Germany, the housing market in London and other big cities had collapsed.

Owner occupation was minimal in the late 1930s, but those with financial means were selling their city homes and moving out to rural areas "just in case".

Prime Minister Chamberlain remained optimistic that hostilities could be averted, but, when the full-scale invasion of Czechoslovakia became likely, he ordered the establishment of Air Raid Precautions (ARP). Cellars and basements were taken over to be turned into shelters and deep trenches were dug in parks.

Ultimately, one of the most terrifying tasks undertaken by members of the ARP was to deal with unexploded bombs.

The safety of children was made the highest priority and Sir John Anderson was invited to co-ordinate a plan to evacuate all of them from our largest cities and into "safe" areas in the countryside.

Many were brought to the rural areas of the north west.

As the inevitability of the Second World War drew near, the Government decided to implement their evacuation plans. Not surprisingly, many youngsters and mothers were deeply upset at being uprooted. Nevertheless, in due course, more than 800,000 school-age children and half a million mothers and children under five went to live in the country.

Teachers - more than 100,000 of them - were also moved out - and thousands of expectant mothers and disabled people also accepted the need to live out of harm's way.

For taking in a child, a householder would receive just over the equivalent of 50p a week from the Government.

Inevitably, standards of hygiene weren't always what they might have been. Headlice and fleas came with many of the youngsters, along with the diseases of deprivation.

The Phoney War, the months immediately following the declaration of war, was a period of uneasy quiet. Naturally, mums and dads were concerned about their children, many of the youngsters were fretting and by Christmas, many of them had been brought back home. Many of the teachers and their families, however, would never return to city life.

Seven months later, the whole process had to be repeated when the Luftwaffe started to bomb our cities.

This time, the Government made arrangements for children to be sent to the United States, Canada and Australia. The scheme was quickly ended when the City of Bernares was sunk by the German Navy - with more than 70 children losing their lives. The start of the air war created the need for warning systems. Sirens were sounded to warn people to take cover and they were sounded again when the danger had passed. Church bells were silenced - to be rung only to warn everyone that the German invasion had begun.

The Government also decided to issue primitive steel shelters named after Anderson which could be erected in people's gardens in areas of risk. Concrete communal shelters also began to appear in residential areas and around schools and other public buildings.

The Morrison shelter, which came later and which was named after the then Home Secretary, was an indoor protective steel cover. Many people simply preferred to crawl under the dining table.

Cities and industrial centres were principal targets for the German bombers but nowhere was truly safe and there were many accounts of indiscriminate raids. In September 1940, a bomber returning from a raid on Liverpool dropped its remaining cargo of death on a fete being held by the Thames Board company in Warrington.

Sixteen people, including children, were killed and more than 50 were seriously injured.

Less than 200 yards away, across the river, thousands of people were watching a Rugby League match at Warrington's Wilderspool Stadium. The incident would lead to a ban on such events in what might be considered targeted areas. The stadium became a storage area for tanks and military equipment until the end of the war.

Air Raid Precautions (ARP) First Observer Corps control room, October 1939

WOMEN AND THE HOME FRONT 1939
July - The Women's Land Army is formed

September 1 - Mass evacuation from towns and cities starts. The Women's Voluntary Service assists with the evacuation

September 2 - National Service (Armed Forces) Act is passed. Men aged 18 to 41 can be called up

Emergency rations for evacuees being distributed, 1939

Rugby players in the Lancashire area, when not on active duty, would "guest" for teams in the more rural areas of Yorkshire.

Such events could not be fully reported by the press…not because morale would be affected but to confuse the Germans as to the effectiveness of their raids.

With a huge Empire providing everything in the way of food and raw materials, the British people lacked nothing before the outbreak of war - except, in so many cases, the money to buy them. Before the Second World War started, Britain imported millions of tonnes of food from our dominions and colonies. To cut the supply line was one of the key priorities of the Germany Navy.

At the start of the hostilities, Britain possessed the world's largest navy - but unfortunately, many of the ships were in a poor state of repair.

The principal Royal Navy bases were Scapa Flow off the northern coast of Scotland and at Portsmouth - and it was from them that the enemy would be taken on at sea. One of the great epic battles began in the Denmark Straits. The British warship Hood was sunk with only three of the 1,421 crew surviving and Germany's most formidable vessel, the Bismarck, also went down, with only 110 sailors cheating a watery grave.

The sinking of the latter marked the end of the Germany Navy's incursions into the Atlantic with visible vessels. At Christmas 1943, by which time the silent enemy in the ocean - the U-Boats - were also retreating to port as detection methods improved. The German Navy would suffer another massive reverse with the sinking of the Scharnhorst, which had been a constant threat to the Russian convoys. Thereafter, more ships of the Royal Navy would be deployed to the Mediterranean and later they returned to the Pacific to support the United States Navy.

Because of the problems with the supply lines, rationing obviously had to be introduced. Householders registered with their neighbourhood shops and books with vouchers were issued.

Inevitably also, the system spawned a whole new economy known as the black market. Dairy produce and meat was more freely available in the country leading to corrupt practices. Someone somewhere could always obtain anything. If a queue began to form at a stall, people would join it without even knowing what was being sold.

Government inspectors would tour shops offering to buy goods without coupons to trap the guilty. The theft of ration books also became widespread.

Nylon stockings had been invented during the year the war broke out and women everywhere flocked to buy them. Because the material could also be used to make parachutes, supplies diminished and there were collections of laddered stockings which could be recycled to make more 'chutes.

Seamed stockings were the ultimate in fashion and when they became unavailable, women would dye their legs and draw lines up the backs.

'Dig for Victory' was a Government initiative which encouraged householders to use their gardens for growing food rather than flowers. Other land was turned into allotments.

Many homeowners also started to keep chickens - and rabbits, goats and pigs.

One of the great fears that civilians held was the Germans would use poison gas. Accordingly, millions of masks were issued. Those for grown-ups were black or brown and looked rather sinister, but youngsters were issued with masks in the shape of Mickey Mouse's face - which helped to take away the scariness of wearing them. Special masks were issued for babies and air raid wardens.

The Government insisted that everyone had to take their gas mask with them wherever they went. Thankfully, the Germans never dropped poison gas.

On the outbreak of war, many civilians too old to serve in the armed forces were anxious to "do their bit" and it was Winston Churchill who suggested to Anderson that a home defence force, which could be trained to defend local communities and key establishments in the event of an invasion, be set up.

Fact file

In public shelters, communal entertainment was often organised. The shared experience of the raids generated spontaneous fellow-feeling. Strangers spoke to each other, neighbours were lavished with cups of tea and publicans gave out free drinks. Class divisions (it seemed) broke down.

December - Over 1.5 million volunteered for the Civil Defence 1940
January - The lack of bombing raids means that two-fifths of evacuees have returned home
June - Over five million women are now in employment
September - The first women are trained to work on anti-aircraft guns
September 7 - The beginning of

Victory in Europe: D-Day and beyond...

A disaster in human terms

Words by Alan Domville

The French port of Dieppe was the scene of the first assault, intended to liberate the continental mainland during the Second World War, by Allied forces.

In terms of military strategy, it was a shambles and, not unexpectedly, it also proved to be a disaster in human terms. Planned in the spring of 1942 by General Bernard Montgomery and Lord Louis Mountbatten, the invasion had been instigated by the Russian leader Joseph Stalin in order to take pressure off the Soviet Union.

The actual invasion had to be delayed until August 19 because of poor weather. Just 1,000 British troops and 5,000 Canadians were landed on the beaches at Dieppe. The Germans were waiting for them and within hours, more than 4,000 had been killed, injured or taken prisoner.

While it was claimed that valuable information

Soldiers preparing to disembark for the D-Day landings

had been gained about the logistics of a future invasion, the number of casualties was appalling. It would be nearly two years before the battle for Europe would begin in earnest.

A more successful operation had been carried out in 1942. German U-Boat raids on Allied shipping bringing food and materials across the Atlantic were causing loss of life and shortages. A daring and successful raid on the dry dock at St Nazaire in France by a 600-strong British commando and naval unit virtually achieved the impossible, rendering it unusable for the rest of the war. Five Victoria Crosses were won on the raid - the largest number ever awarded in a single operation. Gradually, the tide of the Atlantic War turned as our navies were able to better identify the German U-Boats thanks to Enigma's decrypts. And 1943 began with the Russian victory over the Germans at Stalingrad.

The battle was also being taken to the enemy.

THE NORMANDY LANDINGS

D-Day, June 6, 1944

0600 - Sunrise. Aerial bombardment of German fortifications along Utah and Omaha Beaches begins

0630 - American landings begin on Utah and Omaha Beaches

0652 - First reports of conditions on the beaches reach Admiral Ramsay

0700 - German radio broadcast

Landing vehicles come to a halt on the beaches

Fact file

As we can see from this edition of *The New York Times* printed below, the D-Day landings made news

headlines across the globe. Up to 4,000 Allied troops were killed on the first day of battle.

Walls of water swept down the Ruhr and Eder valleys after Wing Commander Guy Gibson's 617 Squadron had breached the dams with the help of Professor Barnes Wallis's bouncing bombs.

Optimists declared that it would be all over by Christmas.

In November, Churchill, Roosevelt and Stalin had met in Teheran and Stalin reiterated his desire for the establishment of a second front in western Europe. Following the disaster of Dieppe, the Prime Minister feared there would be heavy casualties and was reluctant to make any commitment - but after protracted

discussions, it was agreed that an invasion would be planned for 1944.

General Dwight D. Eisenhower, who had led the United States forces in North Africa, was asked to organise Operation Overlord.

This time, it would be an invasion for real. More than one million troops would be mobilised and twice as many personnel would provide essential support services.

It would be the largest invasion force in the history of the world - and when and where it would take place was the best-kept secret of all time.

What couldn't be kept secret was the massive mobilisation of men and machines throughout Great Britain. Holiday resorts, relatively silent for much of the war, came alive as troops were billeted in hotels.

Eisenhower had enlisted his chief of staff, Walter Bedell Smith, Generals Bernard Montgomery, George Marshall and Omar Bradley, Naval Commander Bertram Ramsay, the head of Fighter Command Trafford Leigh-Mallory and Air Marshal Arthur Tedder to co-ordinate the operation.

They planned assaults by British, American and Canadian troops on a 30-mile stretch of coastline comprising five beaches close to the River Orne near Caen and these were given codenames - Sword, Juno, Gold, Omaha and Utah.

The actual attack was preceded by the bombing of bridges across the Seine to disrupt German communications.

Early on June 6 1944, more than 2,700 craft carrying 156,000 troops crossed the Channel. D-Day had arrived. As many again were landed during the following 48 hours.

Artificial harbours called Mulberries had been constructed by civil engineering companies, including Arthur Monk in Warrington and Balfour Beatty, and were towed across the Channel.

Though the German Army had 50 divisions on alert for the expected invasion, Field Marshal Erwin Rommel was actually on leave visiting his family when it began, believing that the Allies would not risk an attack in such bad weather.

General von Runstedt didn't believe the Allied landings were a major operation.

He had decided that the assaults would come between Le Havre and Calais where the Channel was narrower and which would have prevented the allies from fighting their way through so much terrain in Normandy.

When the invasion came Hitler was asleep at his mountain retreat at the Berghof and no one dared wake him.

Up to 4,000 Allied troops were killed on that first day of the battle as a foothold was gained on the continental mainland. Omaha was the most difficult beach to hold.

Hospital ships lying off the coast, manned with medical staff, received their first casualties and staff would work round the clock and round the clock again battling to save lives.

The cities, towns, streets and fields of Normandy would see six weeks of bitter fighting.

The terrain made matters difficult but gradually the Allies moved forward.

Massive support was provided by the parachute troops landing south of St Germain-de-Varreville and near Ste Marie-du-Mont.

initial report of the landing
0710 - US Army 2nd Ranger Battalion begins assault on Pointe du Hoc

0725 - British landings begin on Gold and Sword Beaches
0735 - Canadian landing begins on Juno Beach

0900 - General Eisenhower authorises release of communiqué announcing the commencement of the invasion

Members of the Royal family, above, watch the parade of triumphant troops, below left

Goering's promise to Hitler that no bombs would ever fall on Germany had long been broken, with massive raids on its cities and towns orchestrated by Air Chief Marshal Sir Arthur Harris. In February, a day and night of continual bombardment by Allied air forces on Dresden left 130,000 people dead.
Thirty miles east of Leipzig, at Torgau, on April 25 American and Russian troops shook hands on the broken bridge over the Elbe.
And Russian tanks finally

pounded into the centre of Berlin on April 30.
In the bunker of the chancellery, the cruellest and most despicable dictator of all time took the coward's way out. He shot himself and asked his staff to cremate his body. He knew the Cossacks would have gouged his eyes out and given him the slowest of deaths had they been able to get hold of him.
In the final days, Hitler had been issuing orders to generals who had long ago fled and to armies that no longer existed. Hitler's mistress, Eva Braun, took poison and Goebbels, his chief of propaganda, also died in the bunker.

Grossadmiral Karl Doenitz, who had been certified insane 25 years earlier when he was living in Manchester, had been named by Hitler as his successor.
He was Fuhrer for precisely eight days.
On May 4, General Montgomery received representatives of the German high command in his tent on the bleak Luneburg Heath and accepted their surrender of all their troops in north west Germany, Holland and Denmark. Three days after that, at 2.41 am on May 7, Colonel-General Alfred Jodl, German Army chief of staff, signed the document of unconditional surrender at Rheims.
Victory Day in Europe was organised for May 8 and the Union Flag flew proudly from homes across the nation. In London, on the eve of the day of celebration, Winston Churchill addressed 60,000 people from the balcony of the Ministry of Health in Whitehall and told them: "This is your victory."
The King and Queen and their two daughters, who had remained in London throughout the hostilities, appeared on the balcony of the bomb-damaged Buckingham Palace. The two girls went down into the Mall to join the cheering crowds.
For the first time in almost six years, St Paul's Cathedral was floodlit.
For the moment, Europe was free again - but the World War was not yet over. The conflict in the Far East was still raging and thousands of British soldiers and civilians were still incarcerated in Japanese concentration camps.

reaches the coast at Luc sur Mer between Juno and Sword Beaches. Allied patrols reach the outskirts of Bayeux

2200 - Rommel returns to his headquarters after meetings in Germany. Canadian/British advance on Caen stalls in the

Forest of Lebisay
2207 - Sunset
The Battle for Normandy raged on for two months

Victory over Japan at last...

But not without losses on all sides

Words by Alan Domville

Pearl Harbour, on the Hawaiian island of Oahu, had been used as a base by the United States Navy following the First World War and in the spring of 1940 the fleet was sent there as a warning to Japan, which was threatening aggression in the region.

In the autumn of that year, the Germans and the Japanese signed a peace pact and it is now known that Isouku Yamamoto, commander of the Japanese Fleet, was starting to plan a surprise attack on Pearl Harbour.

Despite various warnings about such an attack, the United States, still isolationist as far as the war in Europe was concerned, did nothing.

On Sunday, December 7, 1941 the unprovoked attack came. More than 300 Japanese military aircraft swept over Pearl Harbour, sinking or destroying 18 warships and hitting almost 200 aeroplanes. Almost 2,000 American troops and civilians were killed. The Japanese announced they were at war with the United

States and Great Britain. Twenty four hours later, a stunned President Roosevelt, supported by the whole of Congress, declared war on Japan.

Within two days, Japanese troops had poured into Malaya, Thailand, Bataan in the Phillipines and the British colony of Burma. In the process of taking Malaya, the Japanese sank the Prince of Wales and the Repulse.

The British Army in Malaya was ill-equipped to cope with the invasion and towards the end of January 1942 its commander, Arthur Percival, ordered a retreat to Singapore. The Japanese gave chase across the Johore Strait and forced Percival's troops to the south of the island. The cause was lost and almost 150,000 British soldiers were taken prisoner.

General William Slim was appointed as commander of all allied troops in Burma in March 1942 but two months later General Alexander ordered a retreat into India.

Early in the following year, Orde Wingate

Fact file

The attack on Pearl Harbour took place on December 7, 1941 under the command of Admiral Nagumo.

The Japanese force consisted of six carriers with 423 planes.

At 6am, the first Japanese attack wave of 83 planes took off. Eighteen US ships were hit during the conflict.

Orde Wingate

(pictured left) came up with a new idea for waging battle. His idea was to fight a terrorist war against the occupiers by destroying military installations and disrupting communications.

His force of 3,000 men were called Chindits, named after the griffin-like mythical beasts which acted as temple guardians in Burma.

Impressed by their success, Churchill agreed with Wingate to expand the size of the Chindit force. Wingate was promoted to Major General and began to plan Operation Thursday - which was aimed at destroying Japanese communications from southern Burma to those that were fighting General Joseph Stilwell and William Slim.

**Pearl Harbour -
Key moments in the build-up to attack**
(with acknowledgements to www.myexecpc.com)

December 7, 1941

0702 - Pte Lockhard and Elliott of Opana Radar Station pick up

what appears to be a flight of unidentified aircraft bearing in 132 miles north of Oahu...discussion follows

General William Slim

In February 1944, Merrill's Marauders attacked the 18th Japanese Division in Burma. This helped Stilwell to gain control of Hakawing Valley. Operation Thursday was launched by Wingate in March 1944. The Chindits set up Broadway, a jungle clearing 200 miles behind the Japanese lines, which included an airstrip so that reinforcements could be flown in and the wounded flown out. Wingate lost his own life in a plane crash that same month.

At the same time, Merrill and his Marauders were continuing to inflict more decisive blows on the Japanese. Again, there were many casualties and Merrill himself suffered a heart attack and also contracted malaria. The Burma war ended two days before the end of the war in Europe when Rangoon was taken by the Fourth Corps led by General Frank Messervy.

In the Philippines, General Douglas MacArthur took his troops to Bataan but was then ordered to Australia. Eleven thousand American soldiers, led by General Jonathan Wainwright, held out for five months. MacArthur was then appointed supreme commander and he and Admirals Chester Nimitz and Ernest King co-ordinated the Pacific fightback.

The Battle of the Coral Sea in May 1942 was technically a draw, for it gave the Americans an advantage at Midway soon afterwards when the Japanese lost all of their aircraft carriers. Guadalcanal in the Solomon Islands was a key to supremacy in the region and there were enormous casualties on both sides before the Americans gained victory. Rabaul, also in the Solomons, was the most important Japanese military base in the Pacific and this fell to the

Americans in 1944.

The battle of Leyte Gulf, part of the liberation of the Phillipines, was the largest military engagement in naval history. The United States Navy destroyed 17 enemy ships in a decisive victory.

Manila was reclaimed in March 1945 and MacArthur turned his attentions towards Okinawa, just more than 300 miles from the Japanese mainland.

A massive defensive effort involved more than 100,000 Japanese troops and 10,000 aircraft. More than 1,300 American ships and more than 150,000 troops were used in an assault as big as that on the Normandy beaches. And, as in the Eurpean offensive, there were massive casualties. The Americans lost more than 12,000 men and the Japanese 10 times as many.

Victory was achieved by the Americans on May 14 and the island's commander, Mitsuru Ushijima, committed hari-kiri.

America now had a base from which to attack Japan but there were fears that in an assault on the mainland there would be thousands more casualties.

In the event, the invasion of Japan never happened. Events taking place thousands of miles away in the New Mexico desert in the United States would change the face of warfare forever.

The possibility that by splitting the atom and involving uranium in the process an explosion many times more powerful than conventional dynamite could be unleashed had been suggested by scientists before the outbreak of the Second World War.

Among them was Lise Meitner, a gifted Jewess who had been dismissed from her university post in Germany and had gone to live in Sweden. Three other scientists who had fled to the United States - Albert Einstein, Leo Szilard and Eugene Wigner - warned President Roosevelt that experiments being carried out in Germany could lead to the creation of an atomic bomb.

Niels Bohr, the world's leading nuclear scientist, was taken to the United States just before the Germans reached his home in Denmark.

Fact file

Enola Gay was a B-29 Superfortress 44-86292 bomber of the US Army Air Force that dropped the atomic bomb on Hiroshima in Japan on August 6, 1945 - just before the end of the Second World

War. The bomber was the single most complicated and expensive weapon produced by the United States during the war.
The atomic bomb was ultimately used against Japan, but it was built as a response to a German threat.
The Enola Gay was assigned to the US Army Air Force's 509th Composite Group and was one of only 15 B-29s modified to deliver nuclear bombs.
Colonel Paul Tibbets, pictured above waving from the plane's cockpit, was the pilot of a crew of 12.
Colonel Tibbets named the bomber after Enola Gay Tibbets, his mother.

0706 - Pte Elliott phones switchboard operator Joseph McDonald at information centre - Ft. Shafter - telling of a large

formation of aircraft approaching the island
0715 - Cpt Outerbridge's attack message, delayed in decoding is

delivered to Duty Officer, 14th Naval District and to Admiral Kimmel's Duty Officer. Japanese launch second wave of 168

Lise Meitner

assault aircraft
0720 - Joseph McDonald, finding Lt Tyler in information centre, calls Opana and patches Lt Tyler through to Pte Lockard who describes the large flight picked up on radar and is told: "Well, don't worry about it."

0733 - Important message from Gen Marshall from Washington to Short received via RCA in Honolulu. Cablegram has

James Franck

Roosevelt had died in the April and had been succeeded by Harry Shippe Truman who had been vice president only since January. On his shoulders fell the decision to drop the bomb on Japan - one of the most awesome in the history of the world.

On the morning of August 6, 1945, a B29 Super Fortress, Enola Gay, armed with the bomb, took off with Commander Paul Tibbets at the controls. Also aboard the plane as an observer was Britain's Group Captain Leonard Cheshire, holder of the Victoria Cross.

Military targets had been selected but, in the event, bad weather meant that the plane was diverted to the industrial city of Hiroshima.

Ninety thousand people were killed as the blinding flash of the atomic detonation was followed by a mushroom cloud of radio active dust towering five miles into the air.

In 1942, the Manhattan Project to develop a nuclear bomb was established at Los Alamos and Brigadier General Leslie Groves brought together the talents of Bohr, Wigner, Szilard, the Americans Robert Oppenheimer and David Bohm, the Hungarian Edward Teller, Felix Bloch from Switzerland, the Italians Emilio Sigre and Enrico Fermi, Britain's James Chadwick and several Germans: Rudolf Peierls, Otto Frisch, James Franck (pictured above) and Klaus Fuchs.

And in all, 100,000 people were involved in the creation of the terrifying new weapon.

While development work moved apace, efforts were also made to disrupt the Germans' own nuclear programme by bombing factories and boats in Norway. They were successful.

The first atomic explosion was not detonated in the New Mexico desert until July 16, 1945, more than two months after Germany had surrendered. Franck and Szilard, stunned by the horror of their invention, called on the government not to use the weapon.

Niels Bohr

Marines and Army infantry faced strong opposition from more than 100,000 troops of Lieutenant General Mitsuru Ushijima's (pictured below) Thirty-second Army.

American intelligence initially estimated Ushijima's strength at only 60,000 to 70,000. Ushijima's naval component consisted of the Okinawa Naval Base Force, the 4th Surface Escort Unit and various naval aviation activities - all under the command of Rear Admiral Minoru Ota.

In this combined command were approximately 10,000 men, of whom only 35 per cent were regular naval personnel. Rounding out the Thirty-second Army was a native Okinawan Home Guard, whose 17,000 to 20,000 members were called Boeitai.

no indication of priority. Messenger Tadao Fuchikami proceeds on normal route 0735 - Reconnaissance plane

from cruiser Chikuma reports main fleet in Pearl Harbour 0739 - Opana Station loses aircraft on radar 20 miles off

coast of Oahu due to 'dead zone' caused by surrounding hills 0740 - First wave sights north shore of Oahu - deployment for

Looking back

"I don't remember how I first heard about the bombing of Hiroshima and Nagasaki; but growing up in Hawaii, there were a lot of mixed feelings about it. Some folks, who once had relatives in Hiroshima or Nagasaki, were very angry at the USA. And some were simply horrified.
I think that history is written by the winners. We'll never know whether the bombing was 'justified'." David Adam Edelstein. Kirkland, Washington, USA.

The Japanese high command immediately dismissed the idea that the Americans had dropped a bomb at all, claiming that it was a freak storm.

Three days later, Truman dispatched a plane to drop another nuclear weapon on the shipbuilding city of Nagasaki. Twenty four hours after that, Emperor Hirohito accepted defeat and the Japanese high command surrendered to General MacArthur aboard the USS Missouri.

The Second World War was over. Fifty five million people had lost their lives.

Or at least the fighting was over. Since the end of the hostilities in Europe, the world had discovered the horrors of the concentration camps in Eastern Europe where it was learned that six million people were slaughtered. Thousands upon thousands of British, Empire and United States troops and civilians had been subjected to unspeakable horrors by the Japanese. Many were simply declared "missing, presumed dead".

All over Europe, millions of battle-weary and homeless people could now set out to rebuild their shattered lives.

The massive task of also rebuilding the infrastructure of a continent devastated by the most destructive battle in history was also beginning but it would take many years for the bomb craters to disappear from scores of cities and towns. In Great Britain, the task of rebuilding society was entrusted not to Winston Churchill but a Labour government. In the General Election of July 5, the result of which was not announced until the 26th because of the need to collate the votes from forces still abroad, Clement Attlee's party won by a landslide. Three hundred and ninety three Labour members would take their places in our bombed Houses of Parliament compared with the Tories' 213. The once-powerful

Liberals won just 12 seats, and there were 22 independents. It was generally felt that Churchill hadn't been rejected personally but people didn't want back in power those who had also rejected him before the war.

Five days after becoming Prime Minister, Attlee attended the resumed conference of the victorious powers in Potsdam and realised that the Russians were preparing to bring down an Iron Curtain on the territories they had "liberated".

A new and different war, the Cold War, had begun.

It would be decades before the barriers came tumbling down and the dream of a truly united Europe would begin to take shape.

attack begins
0749 - Commander Fuchida orders attack...all pilots to begin assault on military bases on

Oahu
0753 - Fuchida radios code to entire Japanese Navy "Tora Tora Tora" indicating

success...maximum strategic surprise. Pearl Harbour is caught unaware...
0755 - Full-scale attack begins

The road to those potatoes wasn't a pleasant one...

"If anyone attempted to strike a match, they were shot at"

Words by Frank Elson

Ernie Holden in warmer and happier times, North Africa 1941

Ernie Holden sat on the deck of The Canterbury, the ship bringing him home from Dunkirk, and peeled potatoes.

"It felt good to be doing something so normal," said the 86-year-old from Farnworth near Bolton. Ernie was one of the lucky ones, evacuated from the beach at Dunkirk. The road that led him to those potatoes was not a pleasant one. "I was conscripted in June 1939 into the Royal Artillery at Hadrian's Camp, Carlisle, finished my training in August and war was declared on September 3. We arrived in Cherbourg in late September and then travelled to Brittany in cattle trucks, 20 men in each truck with a bale of hay to lie on and no washing or toilet facilities except on the stations we stopped at.

'Eventually, about 30 of us were sent to a small village near Arras to join the 13th Field Ambulance (RAMC) as stretcher-bearers. It was a bitterly cold winter with snow on the ground for over a month and we had to make the best of our billets, which were small huts in gardens. There wasn't much military activity except for the odd German recce plane.

'One morning in early May, we were awakened to the sound of explosions. The Germans were bombing Arras and Douai. Word came through that the Germans had invaded Belgium and Holland and we had to advance into Belgium to try to force them back.

There was no fixed battle line at this time as the German Panzer Divisions were very mobile. We rarely stayed in one place for more than two days and had some narrow escapes, just leaving villages before tanks arrived.

The main roads were jammed with civilians trying to get away from the German advance.

'We were retreating towards France and this time there were no cheering people in the streets as there had been when we set off in the other direction. The weather throughout this period had been perfect for the German air force.

They had hundreds of planes, and every one of ours was shot down.

'One day, I was blown in the air by a stick of bombs from a dive-bomber. When things quietened down, we assembled back and found two of our men lying dead in the straw. Up to this time we had been all right but now we were shocked. We buried them together in a corner of a field with their names sealed in a bottle. Afterwards, the Major called us all together and said that we were retreating back to a port in France called Dunkirk. He said that we would travel in the truck and set fire to all the equipment so the Germans couldn't use it. While all this was happening, there were lots of Belgian troops throwing down their rifles in the fields. The King of the Belgians had asked for an armistice with the Germans, so they were no longer fighting. We were ordered to collect these rifles and throw them into the duck pond. I remember them sticking out of the water because we hadn't taken the bayonets off.

'On our way to Dunkirk, I became separated from my mates but managed to get a lift in an ambulance. The town was a shambles as we threaded our way through the bombed streets. Flames licked out of the pavements as the gas mains had ignited and there were dead bodies lying around. We eventually found our way to the dockside. The warehouses had been bombed and all the wounded lay on stretchers in the open with no protection and no sign of a hospital ship. I could see no reason to stay at the docks so I wandered back into the town.

'I met a mate of mine from our company. He seemed in a daze and didn't recognise me. I told him to follow me and try to find a way to the beach and look for a boat. We shambled along until the sand dunes came in sight. I came to the tail end of a queue of troops. There was a lot of tension amongst the men. If anyone attempted to strike a match, they were shot at. Royal Marines were patrolling the queue to stop men sneaking ahead and causing a panic. In fact, I had a narrow escape. I had spotted one of my mates a few yards ahead of me and as I stepped out of the line to have a word, I felt a bayonet prodding my back. I tried to explain that I only wanted a word with my mate just in front, but I had to get back in line smartly. Some Officers had the trick of moving along the queue asking the men if they were all right, but were really making their way to the front of the line. We eventually shuffled to a small gangway on top of the rails. Suddenly I heard a voice shout "13 Field Ambulance," which was my unit. It was one of our officers and he was asking permission for us to come aboard. It seems this ship had been converted to a hospital carrier. It was The Canterbury and it had already done several trips back and forth.

'Eventually, we were out at sea with the pall of smoke of Dunkirk behind us. I was with a pal of mine, Len Brooks, also from Farnworth. We stuck together and when the crew asked for volunteers to peel the potatoes, we sat on the deck with a pile spuds, thankful to be doing something normal."

Ernie, who worked as a miner both before and after World War II, spent four years in North Africa after recovering from Dunkirk.

A prolific local artist, Ernie has completed a number of paintings based on his wartime exploits.

Now lads, I'm afraid it's every man for himself...

"If you want to, you can try to get there. The choice is yours"

Words by Frank Elson

Fred Lee is 86 years old and has many memories of his wartime exploits when he experienced Dunkirk, The Desert War including El Alamein, the Normandy Landings and the occupation of Germany. Now almost blind, Fred, from Horwich, has dictated many of his memories to his niece, Mrs Glennis Aston.

This is Fred's memory of Dunkirk:

"We sailed to France on one of the old Isle of Man steamers. I think it was called the something 'Princess'. We crossed from Dover to Calais and ended up in St Denis. It was quite a pretty little village. I remember a duck pond and a cathedral. The cathedral was fabulous.

'After a few days there, the Germans attacked in Holland and we had to move up to the front line. We travelled through Lille, and into Belgium. The Germans overran us and we had to retreat.

'We were sharing the roads with thousands of refugees, people with carts, hand barrows, anything they could use to carry their belongings. The roads were completely blocked by this human tidal wave so that we couldn't get through in our trucks.

'Eventually, it was decided that we should abandon the vehicles and field guns. I remember we went into a field where a senior Officer told us we would have to spike the guns so that the Germans wouldn't be able to use them.

'A shell was rammed into the breech, then another shell put in behind it, so that the first would explode inside the gun. We had to stand well back as the shell exploded and shattered the barrel. They used lanyards to pull the firing pins so no one got hurt. When we had spiked all the guns, we were told we would have to walk to the coast, to Dunkirk. Everybody was choking for a drink. There was nothing to drink anywhere. When we arrived at Dunkirk, the Germans were shelling the beaches. The only thing we could do was to dig a hole in the sand and get down as low as possible. It gave a bit of protection from shells exploding on the surface. At least we were in a hole. After a couple of hours in these holes, a young subaltern came down the beach.

'He said: "Now lads, I'm afraid it's every man for himself. You can either wade out into the water and try to get onto one of those small boats, or you can try to get to Lepanne. It's about seven miles along the beach. There are two destroyers there. They will wait for you. If you want to, you can try to get there. The choice is yours."

'Another Bolton man and I decided to walk towards Lepanne to try to reach the destroyers. It was hard going, walking through the soft sand, but at last we reached the pier where the destroyers were berthed. There were some military police at the end of the pier. They were very brave men. They stood there as the shells were dropping all round. Still they stood there, directing people, telling them where to go, helping everyone. They told me and my mate to stop. They told us to get down behind the breakwater, which was made of stone. They said they would give us the nod when to run, then we should sprint to the end of the pier and get onto one of the ships as fast as we could. 'Eventually, they gave us the nod, so we ran to the end, to HMS Venomous. A young lad was firing a machine gun at the planes overhead which were dropping bombs. We were still carrying our rifles, so he told us to throw them onboard first. Mine hit the side of the ship and dropped into the water.

'That was terrible. I could have cried. I had struggled with it through seven miles of soft sand, only to lose it like that.

'We were told to go down below, then Jimmy and I sat leaning against a pillar. A young sailor gave us a bottle of brandy and we had a good drink. I think we must have slept a long time, because we woke up in Dover."

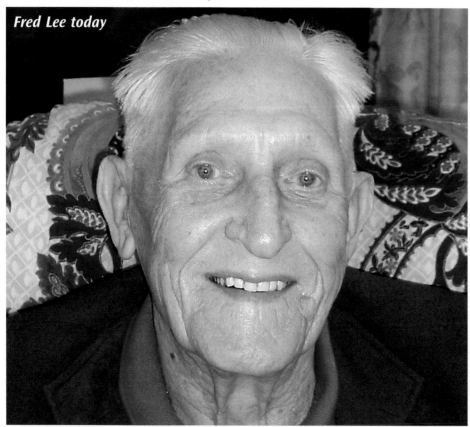

Fred Lee today

From the Vatican to victory

George (second man on the right hand rope, with helmet) moving a field gun during the shelling of German positions on the Yugoslavian mainland in 1944
Right: George Butler today

"I was, as you might expect, completely dumbfounded - a good C of E boy from Bolton with the Pope"

Words by Frank Elson

Wartime throws up some extraordinary stories that do not necessarily involve heroism and fighting. One such story happened to Bolton man George Butler, who now lives, at 84, in Clayton-le-Woods near Chorley. In Mr Butler's own words: "I had to drive some of our lads to Rome for their leave, and I got a couple of days off myself. I was about to go out on the town when I was approached by a Polish Officer who had spotted my 8th Army ribbon and asked me as one 8th Army veteran to another, for a favour.

'His truck had broken down and he needed some way of getting 18 of his lads into Rome. I was going myself anyway so I agreed. I drove into the City; this was within a few weeks of peace being declared, following his directions until we got to the Vatican walls. I stopped but he waved me on, showing some paperwork to the guards. 'Eventually, we came to a stop inside the Vatican City itself and they started to get out. I was staying where I was but the Officer told me to come with them. We then went on a tour of the Vatican with a real guide explaining it all until we ended up in a room on our own. There was a lot of noise outside, orders being shouted and the like, and in marched a bunch of Swiss Guards, complete with pikes, who took up station in front and behind us. Then the Pope was carried in in a sedan chair! He spoke to the soldiers. They told me later that he was congratulating them on their bravery at Monte Cassino (these were the lads who had carried out the final assault) and then turned and congratulated me as well, but in English!

'I was, as you might expect, completely dumfounded- a good C of E boy from Bolton with the Pope. But the really funny thing about all of this is that I hadn't been at Monte Cassino. At the time of the assault, I was away in Yugoslavia raiding Germans and, amongst other things, watching Tito dance with the locals and you can't get anyone much more un-Pope-like than a communist leader!"

George had an interesting war in more ways than one, including the way he joined up. As a fresh-faced 18-year-old working for "a 50 bob tailor" in Bolton, George was, one evening, a member of a winning darts team. "Everyone decided to celebrate a great victory and proceeded to get well-oiled, except me because they wouldn't serve me. I was stone-cold sober but rather carried away with the excitement when we all joined the 53rd Field Regiment of the Royal Artillery that night!

'Of course, I had intended on joining up at some stage, so the next day, when my father wanted to rescind my membership and "give them their shilling back," I wouldn't let him and instead went off to serve for seven years in the Army."

And, after a varied career at Dunkirk, North Africa, Sicily, Italy, Yugoslavia and Greece, during which he became part of the 111th Field Regiment, his homecoming in 1946 was not without interest either.

"When you were demobbed, you could get your old job back, so I did. The man who had my job at the time was Glynn Owen, who died recently. He was so miffed at losing the job that he went off to London and started his career as an actor."

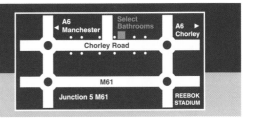

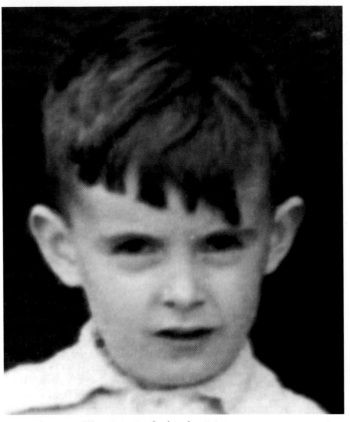

Roger McCallister, aged six, in 1943

Mr McCallister today, aged 67

I knew nothing else, only war...

"I remember rations, blackouts, Dad's allotment, dandelion and burdock, friends' fathers absent for long periods, American airmen dropping sweets from their trucks as they passed our primary school"

Words by Frank Elson

Those born just before the start of World War II grew up knowing nothing else. Roger McCallister was born in 1937 and lived at Bolton Road, Atherton.

He writes: "As a child, I was not afraid of the war. I accepted it for six years as the normal way of life. I had known nothing else. My earliest memories in life are of air raid sirens and my mother taking me from my bed to shelter under the stairs. My father, who worked at Walker's Tannery, Bolton, was regularly out at night with the Home Guard. Later, we acquired a Morrison Shelter which was basically a metal reinforced dining room table. It was under that table one night in 1940 or 1941 that I still recall one of the most vivid memories of my life.

'The Germans dropped a bomb on the farmyard near Atherton Central Station. Presumably they were aiming for the railway. I can still hear the tinkle of glass as our windows came in and scattered glass over the tabletop under which I was sheltering. The next day, my mother took me to see the hole in the farmyard where all the livestock had been killed and the shattered remains of houses along Bolton Road.

'I was bewildered as to why anyone should want to cause so much destruction and was told that it was nasty Germans. In my child's mind, I thought of all Germans as evil monsters; an impression that lasted until well after the war when I saw Bert Trautmann in goal for Manchester City at Burnden Park.

'I have been told since that if that row of houses had not been there to take the main blast of the bomb, our house just to the rear on the opposite side of the railway would probably have collapsed and I would probably not have survived. I was also taken to see even greater scenes of devastation in central Manchester after bombing. We had been able to see the fires at night from Atherton.

'I remember rations, blackouts, Dad's allotment, dandelion and burdock, friends' fathers absent for long periods, American airmen dropping sweets from their trucks as they passed our primary school. I especially remember my first sight of a banana, brought home by my sailor uncle. We gazed at it in wonder at a family gathering in Deane.

'When we had victory bonfires in the back street in 1945, I do remember a feeling of excitement at the prospect of better days. There was a great communal togetherness then that I have never experienced since."

What is a hero anyway?

"We took ammo off the bodies as well. They didn't need it and we did"

Words by Frank Elson

It is the odd, almost funny things that stick in Ron Ashmore's mind. As part of a group of airborne troops held up a few miles from Arnhem itself, Ron had to dig in near to a nice house.

"I asked the elderly lady who lived there if I could borrow her spade and she let me have it, but asked us to be careful of her vegetables - well they had nothing to eat, did they?

'Anyway, the next day after a German bombardment, she didn't have a house left. I know it's not really funny, but we did find a sort of gallows humour in the situation."

Ron, from Belmont near Bolton, was a Sergeant in the... "now get this right young man, the 7th Battalion, King's Own Scottish Borderers, 1st

Ron Ashmore the day after he and his comrades rejoined the Allies

Airborne Division."

"It's a mouthful, isn't it? I was called up in 1940, spent three months at Lancaster and then went to the 7th Battalion in the middle of the night somewhere down south. I woke up the

next morning on a beach and thought I was among foreigners. At 25 years of age, I was hearing Scottish people talk for the first time in my life!"

Not a Paratrooper, Ron was glider-borne.

"We missed D-day because we were training, always training. Landing a glider wasn't easy. We lost more than one in training; that was with around 25 young men inside."

In fact, on the first day of Operation Market Garden, the supposedly difficult landing went well.

"We were a bit scattered but rallied to the sound of the piper. We were the first to land. Our job was to clear the ground for the Paras, otherwise they would just get shot as they floated down. Of course it all went wrong because of the Panzers. Just plain bad luck that they were in the area.

'Airborne-land with just light weapons, a few mortars, hardly any food or provisions and just enough ammunition that you can carry. Oh, we did have some small handtrucks to pull some ammunition along. The idea was to hold the area, get reinforced by the Paras, march to Arnhem and then hang on for the ground troops' breakthrough.

'Of course, we ended up fighting from the moment we landed. We fought as far as Oosterbeek. It was dirty house-to-house fighting and we were held there. We weren't going anywhere, not against tanks. That's where I borrowed the spade. We had no equipment for things like trench digging."

Using petrol bombs they scavenged, mortars and bunches of hand grenades tied together, against the odds, the airborne troops did destroy a few tanks. They also repulsed a lot of German infantry attacks.

"We were stuck where we were, in action almost constantly and the clock was ticking. There was confusion and some of our lads went a bit strange- you know, they couldn't take it.

'One night, someone came up to us talking in a guttural tone. I wouldn't shoot him because we tried not to give our positions away in the dark and I was working on another way of killing him when something he said made me realise it was one of my own lads who had been shot in the throat. So then I took him to the first aid station. I saw things there that I could never tell people about, really bad injuries, and then I made my way back.

'Moving across this field, some Germans whispered to me to come and give myself up. They had to be kidding! I marked their position, got back to my lads and then, at first light, we

attacked and took them prisoner instead!

'We ate fruit from orchards and dug up turnips and things to eat. I did get a bit miffed when I found the Officers sitting in a cellar eating off china plates though.

'There was a Captain who was a bit... well... he called to me one day and told me to throw this boot away. It had a foot in it and he didn't like it there in front of his position. Of course, I crawled out, grabbed it and heaved it. In the main though, the officers were in the same boat as us, stuck and being shot at. A lot.

'Mind you, we did a bit of shooting back. I was a Marksman and all I'll say is that I did my bit to even the odds. Here's another daft one. Our MO made a deal with the Germans that if we withdrew from the first aid station, they would come in and look after our wounded men. The MO had nothing left for them at all, so all the able-bodied men withdrew. Then our CO sent me back to see if any of the wounded were good enough to fight. I got there and the MO, waiting for the Germans, blew a fuse. He told me to get back as they would shoot me, being able-bodied.

'I was getting fed up with this to-ing and fro-ing. I had to crawl through houses, under cover all the time, and in one of them I spotted all this shaving gear, so I thought "nuts to them" and stopped and had a shave.

'Funny what you remember. I really don't remember when exactly I was wounded. It was a shell burst and it took away a bit of my knee. You can still feel the hole today. You didn't use your own bandage in case you needed it later, so I took one from a body nearby and carried on."

Today, Ron is a sprightly 90 with twinkling eyes that cloud momentarily as some memories come to him. He does wonder why he came home when so many didn't.

"I wonder why I was spared. I have always tried to be nice to people. Even as a Sergeant I wasn't one of those who shouted and screamed. I'd ask... and my lads fought and sometimes died because I asked them to.

I also went with them most of the time. We weren't heroes, we were tough and we were well trained and we did the job they asked us to do and then some.

'They told us three days; we were there for nine, but heroes?

What is a hero anyway? I came back home and worked in the bleachworks.

'The war, Holland, was a very long time ago, but still sometimes, in the night, I think about it."

Trevor before being taken prisoner

Trevor Mellows

Thrown to the wolves...

"One thousand of us went out to the island, only 250 got back"

Words by Frank Elson

Trevor Mellows does not hate the Japanese. At 86 years of age and with his health ruined by three-and-a-half years of captivity, he admits to being bitter. But he cannot find it in himself to hate his gaolers.

"I am bitter about what happened. My health has been bad ever since the war, all as a result of dysentery," he said. "I don't hate them though, and I certainly don't hold anything against the young Japanese today. I can't even begin to understand their psyche though. Those that had us in the camps were incredibly cruel people. I have never been able to understand their apparent need for cruelty for its own sake."

Trevor, who actually escaped from Singapore before the fall only to be captured a few weeks later, is also still angry about the British war effort- or lack of it- that led to the fall of Singapore.

"Churchill sacrificed us. He knew what was happening and he let it happen to help bring the United States into the war. It's only now that the full story is coming out, about British deserters and the like. I for one don't blame them. We were in no state to oppose the Japanese at all."

Trevor joined the RAF straight from Bolton County Grammar School. By the time he was 23 and on his way to Singapore, he was an experienced aircraftsman.

"We were actually on board ship when war was declared in 1939. When the Japanese were overrunning Singapore in 1942, I was on one of the last ships out. We went to Java, where we were taken prisoner when the Dutch capitulated."

Trevor then spent three-and-a-half years as a prisoner of the Japanese, mainly on an island near to New Guinea.

"We were very badly treated. I am lucky to be alive. One thousand of us went out to the island, only 250 got back."

Trevor's closest friend and another former POW, Hughie Dewhurst, moved to Staines from the Halliwell home he grew up in some years ago. Both men admit to feeling let down by a combination of the British Government and the Singapore authorities.

Mr Dewhurst said: "The whole theatre of operations in the Far East was a shambles. It has been proven time and again. The people out there, servicemen and civilians, were completely misled right down the line. We even read stories in the Straits Times about how the Japanese could not bomb Singapore because their eyesight wasn't good enough! In fact, the Japanese were better equipped and better trained than we were. We were thrown to the wolves for political reasons." Hughie and Trevor crossed paths frequently throughout the war and during their captivity.

"I got out of Singapore on February 13, two days before the fall on the Empire Star," added Hughie.

"We went to Java where we were captured on March 8. Trevor and I served on the same base in Malaya. We kept bumping into each other in prison camps and then ended up travelling back to Bolton on the same train!"

Hughie also suffered from the cruelty of his captors.

"They treated us as expendable. The mortality rate was 60 per cent. At one time, I was transferred between two islands on the Maros Maru, a 600-ton freighter. We were on deck in all the elements for 69 days with very little food, just a handful of rice now and again, and restricted water. Of the 650 of us who set off, only half survived the trip. People died from a combination of cruelty and neglect."

Now 83, Hughie cannot hate the Japanese, as it was "all too long ago," but he is sad that the Japanese do not admit their guilt.

"They do not teach their own youngsters about what happened. They've deleted it from their history books. Young people should know so that it could never happen again."

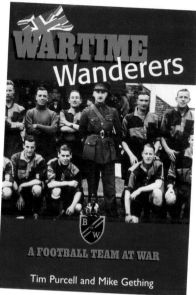

Stories of bravery, patriotism... and football

"Written from first-hand accounts, Army diaries and contemporary reports in the Bolton Evening News, Wartime Wanderers is a completely factual book that tells the story as it happened"

Words by Frank Elson

In 1943, an Iraqi football team due to play against a British Army team in Persia turned up without boots. After a quick discussion, the British Army team decided that rather than risk injuring their opponents by tackling while wearing their boots, they would play in bare feet as well! Naturally, with a team consisting mostly of former Bolton Wanderers players, despite their handicap, the British won.

That is just one of the extraordinary stories contained in the book Wartime Wanderers, which chronicles the story of the 15 Bolton players who joined the Army en masse just before the start of the Second World War.

It is a story of bravery, of patriotism and of football. And it is also the story of how, when faced with a morning dash across a frozen field for a shave and a wash, the fitter former Wanderers always won!

The book, written by Tom Purcell and Mike Gething, has unsurprisingly, been a bestseller in Bolton for years.

In early 1939, anyone with any sense could see that a war with Germany was almost inevitable. Britain was preparing for war, albeit a little late.

On Monday afternoon, April 10, 1939, Sergeant Bill Killan was on duty at the Territorial Army recruitment office in Bradshawgate when the entire Bolton Wanderers first team led by captain Harry Goslin walked in and signed up for the 53rd Field Regiment of the Bolton Artillery.

It was a patriotic and brave move of course, but tempered with some common sense, as the players were well aware that if they waited for conscription, they could have been split up and sent wherever the War Office decided.

By joining together, they virtually ensured that they would stay together in the same unit. This they did. The 15 players who signed that day went through the war in the same unit-although only 14 returned.

Written from first-hand accounts, Army diaries and contemporary reports in the Bolton Evening News, Wartime Wanderers is a completely factual book that tells the story as it happened.

It is also the story of the younger Wanderers and club officials who were left behind, and of the pain and problems of trying to run a football league of sorts in wartime conditions. It includes the story of a 14-year-old Nat

Lofthouse, who on Saturday was climbing a drainpipe at Burnden Park to catch a glimpse of his heroes and, the following Monday, was signing apprenticeship forms for the club. The young man's confusion would be apparent to anyone. On the day he signed to play for the Wanderers, the entire team left to join the Army!

Dunkirk, El Alamein and the bloody fighting up the eastern coast of Italy are, to many of today's Wanderers fans, tales from the history books.

The Wartime Wanderers were there in the thick of the fighting often covered in mud, baked by the desert sun but always, whenever and wherever conditions allowed, digging those football boots out of their kitbags and playing a game.

From a desert kickabout to an almost fully-fledged international match against the Polish Army, one thing is certain, never before and almost certainly never again has one British Army Unit been able to field such a strong Regimental Team!

Wartime Wanderers- A Football Team At War, is published by Mainstream Publishing at £7.99, ISBN 1-84018-583-X.

One hero's recollections of those war years

**Above: William Yates during the war with his hard-working motorcycle.
Right: William shortly before his death in 2000.**

"Some of these had been hit by the German 88mm armour piercing shells which exploded and burned the poor tank crew to a cinder"

Words by Frank Elson

William Yates died in August 2000, aged 82. He wrote down some of his memories of World War II shortly before his death. His son, Graham Yates, of Bradshaw, Bolton, said: "My own belief is that everyone who lived during those war years is a hero."

This then, is a part of one hero's recollections:

"I was called up on January 17, 1940, to join the South Lancs Infantry Regiment. After initial training, myself and other men who had motorbike licences were formed into a motorcycle platoon. Our job was to look out for any signs of enemy paratroops and any sign of a German invasion."

From that time, William found himself transferred around until eventually he joined the Royal Electrical Mechanical Engineers where he became a Corporal.

"After D-Day, our landing day was D6 so we had an easy landing. We had to start on our job of recovery, bringing away from the battle area the tanks which had been put out of action. Some of these had been hit by the German

88mm armour piercing shells which exploded and burned the poor tank crew to a cinder. We had to go inside the tanks and remove what bits were left of them.

'The German resistance was eventually overcome from around Caen and the surrounding area, and their retreat was so comprehensive that when we were told we were on the move, we were also told to fuel up for 200 miles. Then we drove through France and into Belgium.

'At one point, myself and Fred, a driver, had to go to a certain bridge and be on standby in case anyone got stuck there holding traffic up. We would have to pull them out of the road. We were there on our own for a few days and slept in the truck before a Belgian family who lived near the bridge made us welcome in their house.

'So then we took it in turns for one of us to stay the night in their house and have supper and a lovely bed and the other one to stay in the truck. Later, we moved into Holland to a town called Eindhoven, where we were quite settled for a while until the Germans mounted a

counter attack. That was the Battle of the Bulge in the Ardennes.

'The next move I remember was to a place called Falingbostal in Germany itself. While in that area, I had to go on my motorbike to the village of Belsen where one of our units was stationed and of course rode round the outside walls of the infamous concentration camp to see for myself what I had been hearing about.

'On the grass verges surrounding the camp I saw some of the former inmates lying about on the grass. Some of them, I was told, used to go to our unit's cookhouse for scraps of food, and even scraped what they could out of thrown away empty food tins.

'Our next move was to our final destination in Oldenburgh where I was given the job, along with a Sergeant and four lads, of running a park for removing useful parts from broken down vehicles. At this time I had a little rough-haired terrier dog I called Rags. He followed me everywhere and would jump straight into my jeep. I did this job until I left the Army, and the only thing that upset me about leaving was having to leave Rags behind."

With colleagues during the war. Peter is on the back row, far left

Peter and Stella with a card illustrated by an Italian Peter befriended

Lest we forget those who did not come home to their sweethearts

"Mind you, in the pitch black with the enemy goodness knows how close, you did wonder"

Words by Frank Elson

Peter Hodgkinson left his sweetheart, Stella, on the platform at Bolton station when he went to war in February, 1941.

He arrived back in August 1945 to find her standing on the same platform.

Although, as a Royal Engineer, Peter was not directly involved in fighting, he was often on the battlefield as the fighting raged around him. Perhaps his most dangerous experience was during the second night of the Battle of El Alamein.

"We had to clear paths through the minefields," said Peter, aged 83. "We laid white tape to show the path and marked the mines for our colleagues behind to defuse. It wasn't frightening, it was just something we did."

Then he smiled: "Mind you, in the pitch black with the enemy goodness knows how close, you did wonder. I was never 100 per cent sure about those mines."

For Peter, the main memory of Alamein is of noise and dust.

"We knew when the first barrage was to start and we all stood in the dark waiting. When they opened up, it was the biggest roar you could imagine. We weren't on sand, it was all rocks and stones, but every vehicle threw up clouds of dust. Everything was covered in it."

Towards the end of the battle and just afterwards, Peter was involved in rebuilding the pipeline that carried water for most of the length of the North African coastal road.

"One thing about the desert is that you really appreciate how precious water is."

Peter is a committee member of the Bolton Branch of the 8th Army Veterans Association Together with many of his old comrades and his wife Stella, Peter attends remembrance ceremonies for the war and for Alamein.

"Lest we forget those who did not come home to their sweethearts."

So many stories, so many memories...

Walter Woods and the medals he earned all those years ago

"Well he won't be walking home. He was in a body bag"

Words by Frank Elson

Walter Woods marched in his first Remembrance Day Parade in 1948, just a few years after World War II ended.

At the time, Walter's memories were still vivid of men he had known as friends and watched die. Today, Walter's memories have dimmed somewhat with age, but he is still as fiercely determined as ever that they should be remembered.

Walter will be carrying the Standard of the Bolton Combined Ex-Servicemen's and Women's Association in Bolton as long as he is able. He is the vice chairman of that organisation and treasurer of the Normandy Veterans' Association. "We combined a few years ago because all the associations, Burma Star, 8th Army and the others were getting short of people," he said. A spry 85-year-old, Walter believes that we should always have a Remembrance Day, so long as there is a soldier alive who fought and watched his comrades die. "There are still men alive who fought in World War I and we should always have a parade for them all."

Walter joined the Territorial branch of the 5th Battalion of the Loyal Regiment in 1938 because he could see a war was looming. In typical Army fashion, he then found himself moving around and ended up serving with the 6th Battalion, the 2nd Recce Corps, "riding high speed motorcycles out in front of the main Army, just like the Germans did," the Royal Army Ordinance Corps and finally the Royal Electrical and Mechanical Engineers (REME). "I wasn't sure what I was after a while," he smiled. Having helped train some of the men who went on to the Normandy beaches on D-Day, Walter himself was on board a ship just off the coast on that fateful day.

In fact it was eight days later before he and his party scrambled ashore to fight their way across France and into Germany. He ended the war in Hanover.

"There are so many stories and so many memories," he said, "like the ship that hit a mine just off the beach. Every soldier and sailor on board died before they even stepped on to the sand."

One of the most poignant memories is of 16-year-old Private Banks from Darwen.

"Somehow, he'd managed to join up, despite his age. His family found out and started hunting for him. Finally, they found out where he was and petitioned the War Office to get him out. So one day, the CO was reading out the orders to send him back home to the RSM, who turned round and said: "well he won't be walking home." He was in a body bag."

Walter has been back to France and seen Private Banks's grave in a War Cemetery. He has also carried the Normandy Vets Standard during a D-Day Commemoration parade in Normandy. It is for people like Private Banks that Walter insists that Remembrance Day must continue.

"There were more than 200 of us at that first parade in 1948," he said. "I was there to remember all those I had known who were killed, but of course, it became more than that. Whether we knew them or not, they must be remembered. I want to know why children are no longer taught about the war in schools. In Holland, children are taught in the schools and every year they plant flowers in honour of those who fought at Arnhem. They won't forget, will they?"

I thought I would live forever...

Bill Smith shows off the medal and certificate he received at a ceremony in Normandy on the 50th anniversary of D-Day

"My mate was in a boat next to us. I watched it get blown clean out of the water"

Words by Frank Elson

As the motor launch carrying Bill Smith approached Sword Beach in Normandy, German officers came out of their homes to gaze in bewilderment. Bill said: "They were in a state of undress and were obviously not expecting us. Unfortunately, it didn't last. The bullets started to fly pretty quickly and our boat was peppered with shrapnel. It was one of the weirdest things that happened." Not so amusing was the fate of one of Bill's mates, Scot John Mackie. The two had been through training together. "He was in a boat near to us," said Bill, speaking at his Bolton home. "I watched it get blown clean out of the water." Bill was a 19-year-old wireless telegraphist and joined the Navy at the beginning of the war. The last thing he expected, with a job like his, was to be one of the very few Bolton men to land in Normandy during the invasion. "It wasn't what I had planned," he said. "But I knew it was coming. I had been transferred to Combined Ops, training for the invasion for a while." As the crew of a pilot boat, Bill and his colleagues were sitting in the middle of the English Channel on the evening of June 4, 1944. "The weather was appalling. We were being thrown around in this tiny boat, waiting to guide some landing craft on to the beach.

That was the night the invasion was cancelled due to the weather and we were told to wait out there!

'The next day, we did get a start though. We were leading Number 4 Commando, the ones with Lord Lovatt commanding, and were heading for a small town called Ouistreham. And taking the Germans by surprise meant they had a quieter landing than on other beaches. Those German officers were really surprised to see us at first, but when they woke up it got very noisy very quickly.

'We were told later that the gun doing most of the damage, including to my mate's boat, was one of those Big Bertha things firing from Le Havre." Bill's arrival on the beach, along with the first British troops to land, was smooth enough. "All I had was my radio equipment, no weapon, so I couldn't even fire back. I had to set up on the beach to pass messages back and forth. A Commando Sergeant took pity on me and threw me a shovel so I dug a hole and sat in it, listening to the bullets flying overhead and the groans of injured men lying nearby. I wasn't frightened as such. I was 19. I thought I would live for ever and, anyway, there was too much to do." There were also some personal moments that stuck with Bill. "I landed in the early morning of June 6 and in the afternoon, I was drinking a glass of wine in a wine cellar in

Ouistreham! There were three women sitting in a corner with scarves over their heads. The bar girl told us they had their heads shaved for collaborating with the Germans, so the French hadn't wasted any time. I felt sorry for them really. How would any of us have behaved under occupation? It was about survival really. 'On the 7th, we sailed back to Portsmouth and handed over all our messages. I had been on watch since the 4th. I needed a rest."

Shortly afterwards, Bill was sent to the Pacific where he remained until VJ day, August 14, 1945. "I sailed right around the world. We left Liverpool during the war, went to America, down and through the Panama Canal, up to the Philippines, then Japan, Singapore, through Suez and the Med and then back home after the war had finished in June 1946." A father of four with eight grandchildren and one great-grandchild, Bill does not dwell on the war years, particularly the historic D-Day landings. "I was one of just three Bolton men who landed in Normandy on the first day. I know it was important now but at the time, it was just something that had to be done. 'You were a young man on a beach with bullets flying around and you did your job. We thought that this was the war to end all wars but it seems as though there has been nothing but war since. We thought the world would be at peace."

The young David Yates when he served in the Navy

David Yates today

Under heavy fire, we managed to get all 10 men on board...

"The vessel was leaking burning oil which threatened to engulf the screaming men"

Words by Frank Elson

Many soldiers, sailors and airmen received medals throughout the war. This is the story of one sailor who won a medal along with his entire crew. David Yates, now aged 81 and living in Kearsley, Bolton, was part of the crew of an LCS (Landing Craft Support) that was awarded the Distinguished Conduct Medal after the landings at Salerno, Sicily. Mr Yates was a member of Combined Operations and crewed an LCS which was launched from the decks of the converted cross channel ferry Princess Astrid along with a number of LCAs (Landing Craft Assault). He said: "The assault vessels that Princess Astrid carried, LCAs and the LCS that I was aboard, were launched from her decks and formed part of a larger

force that was to land troops and armoured vehicles on the occupied beaches of Salerno. 'Under heavy fire and bombardment, the landing started and troops, together with tanks and armoured vehicles, started to hit the shore so that they could form a beachhead in readiness for the land battle. As one of the LCAs started to come astern from the beach, it was hit by defensive shore artillery and quickly burst into flames. The crew of 10 had no option but to evacuate into the water to avoid the exploding ammunition that was still on board. Unfortunately the vessel was leaking burning oil which threatened to engulf the screaming men. Due to the fact that our LCS was all steel, it was decided that there was no other course of action but to form a physical

barrier between the burning oil and the men in the water. Under heavy fire, we managed to get all 10 men on board and eventually, safely onto a Red Cross ship. We completed our mission and stayed at Salerno for six or seven days before being taken back aboard an Australian ship, the Fort Kilner, to our parent ship HMS Princess Astrid in Valetta Harbour, Malta. As we were lowered from the decks of the Fort Kilner and made our way to the Astrid, we were amazed to see the crews of all the other ships lining the decks in a formation known as 'standing to.' As we boarded the Astrid, we were told that our LCS had been awarded the DCM as a result of saving the lives of the 10 crewmen of the burning LCI while in danger from heavy enemy fire."

After an uneventful 30 hour crossing...

"When the war in Europe ended in May 1945, the anti-tank platoon had 13 men left of the original platoon of 33"

Words by Nick Nunn

Walter Bretherton, of Bannister Lane, Eccleston, is chairman of Chorley and District ex-Services Association. He recalls the conflict immediately after the D-Day landings and his service in France, Belgium, Holland and Germany.

"June 6, 1944 found me going aboard an LST (Landing Ship Tank) at Southsea Harbour, Portsmouth, with a unit of the Royal Electrical and Mechanical Engineers.

"Our job was to make sure that any vehicle that had broken down or been damaged by enemy action was cleared from the beach or road from the beach and if possible get the vehicle moving again. We landed on Sword Beach, a short distance from the town of Ouistreham near Caen on the second day, June 7, after an uneventful 30 hour crossing. The sea was very rough and to take my mind off seasickness, I volunteered to man an anti-aircraft gun hoping for some action.

"After about two weeks, our services were no longer required as the battle had moved on and REME workshops were beginning to arrive. I received orders that I was to proceed to the 2nd Battalion Gordon Highlanders. The Gordons had suffered heavy casualties in their first engagement and were being reinforced for Operation Epsom, which was designed to drive inland and deepen the existing bridgehead. I found myself joining the anti-tank platoon.

"I stayed with the Gordons through all the battles across Belgium and Holland into Germany and the awful Bergen-Belsen concentration camp. By May 1945, we were east of Lubeck and near the Baltic coast where we met up with the Russian forces. After a few weeks of occupying Lubeck, we were ordered back to England to undergo training for the invasion of Japan. Fortunately, from our point of view, the decision was taken to drop the atom bomb on Japan and the invasion was no longer necessary, thus saving many thousands of allied lives. When the war in Europe ended in May 1945, the anti-tank platoon had 13 men left of the original platoon of 33. In addition, some of the replacement also became casualties in turn, and the final total was 41. The Rifle Platoons suffered even more. The 15th Scottish Division was always in the forefront of the campaign in North West Europe and suffered a higher than average casualty rate. They were singled out by General Montgomery and praised for their distinctive achievements. About thirty per cent of the division were English."

Above: Walter Bretherton wears his medals with pride. Below: Back in those perilous days after the D-Day landings

A French hero relives a Blackburn soldier's 'Great Escape'

Charlie Jones in action
Inset: Charlie with his daughter

"I was captured and was taken prisoner by the Germans. When I returned, all my family were dead - two sisters and my mother. It was a dangerous time"

Words by Nick Nunn

A French soldier has relived the moment he helped a teenage squaddie from Blackburn escape the Germans after they invaded. André Buzin, aged 78, was living in Béthune, north of Bordeaux on the west coast of France and welcomed Charlie Jones into his house for three weeks in Christmas 1939.

His appeal for information about the young soldier he helped to escape has resulted in Charlie's daughter Barbara Thompson, aged 60, of Beatrice Place, Blackburn, coming forward. Barbara unearthed some of the letters and photographs sent between the two men, and she revealed for the first time to André the "full life" Charlie was able to lead thanks to his escape. Tragically, Charlie, a dad of two and granddad of five, died suddenly on Father's Day 18 years ago aged 68, a year after retiring. He lived at Wellington Street, Accrington and worked in a moulding shop and at Huncoat Power Station until he retired.

Speaking from Bezier in France, André reminisced about the events of 1939.

After three years of mounting international tension, Hitler invaded Poland on September 1. Three days later, the allies declared war on Germany, which meant British troops were on the Continent for Christmas.

Andre said: "We were asked by the Mayor to welcome three soldiers into our farm for Christmas. My mother agreed and I spent the time with Charlie, teaching him how to drive and maintain the tanks in the garage. I was only 14 at the time. But one night, the Germans had sneaked up the river all the way to its mouth and got out of kayaks. They hid in the bushes. When we realised, I helped Charlie get to Bordeaux by train where he could get a boat to safety. I was captured and was taken prisoner by the Germans. When I returned, all my family were dead- two sisters and my mother. It was a dangerous time. It is sad to hear Charlie died. It's a shame. But it is also very good news to hear that he went on to be happy. I so, so wanted to hear from him again."

The Nazi advance gathered pace after the Christmas of 1939 and France signed an

armistice with them on June 22, 1940. André was not released until France was liberated in August 1944.

Charlie was an artillery soldier during the war. He married Olive Jones, now aged 87 of Oswaldtwistle, when he was 21.

Barbara said: "He didn't often talk about the war because I think he saw a lot of things he didn't want to repeat. But he loved his time with André in France. He used to come out with French phrases a lot and we never really knew where they were from.

"I was clearing out some cupboards and found this bundle of letters and photographs from France. It is a shame my dad is not alive to be reunited with André but at least now he knows Charlie went on to lead a full and happy life." The letters are dated between January and December 1945. They are addressed to Charlie and signed from 'Your Friends of France'. They request news from Charlie and invite him to spend more time in Béthune as well as detailing the relief that the four-year occupation was coming to an end.

Some of the world's most dangerous oceans...

"I was only 18 and full of adrenaline but when I noticed the faces of the adults on board, they looked very afraid"

Words by Caroline Innes

For an 18-year-old runaway, joining the Merchant Navy seemed like an exciting adventure that would take him to every corner of the world.

But as the Second World War broke out, Cliff Westell found himself charged with the vital task of keeping Britain supplied with food and arms.

He told Caroline Innes about sailing across some of the world's most dangerous oceans, being shot at by enemy aircraft and how an onboard friendship inspired him to follow a career in local politics.

Cliff Westell is one of the lucky ones.

Mr Westell as a young man

One in three men who sailed away with the Merchant Navy during the Second World War were killed at sea.

The heavily armed ships, tasked with such an important role, were often protected by convoys of aircraft carriers as they ferried precious supplies to Britain from across the world.

But attacks on the fleets that were Britain's only lifeline were common, and relative to its size, the Merchant Navy sustained more casualties than any other service.

Cliff said: "We were part of a five-ship convoy and only 12 hours out of Gibraltar when we were attacked by aircraft. The bombs were literally just missing us and the splash from them as they hit the ocean swamped the deck with water.

"We had an aircraft carrier in escort and immediately they sent up their Seafires which were the naval equivalent of Spitfires. As I sat in my harness behind a concrete guard, watching the dogfight that was going on above me and shooting a twin gun at the enemy, it just felt as if I was watching a picture - I didn't feel scared because it just didn't seem real.

"I had been arms trained by a Marine but my firing was not good and I think our pilots were in more danger than the enemies. I was certainly closer to the tail of our Seafires than theirs. I was only 18 and full of adrenaline but when I noticed the faces of the adults on board, they looked very afraid and I realised what a near-miss we had just experienced."

Despite the drama of an air bomb attack, Cliff who was born in 1922 in Church and now lives in Clayton-le-Moors with wife Dorothy, said his most memorable experience of the war was on his very first trip to New York.

There he would meet a man who would inspire Cliff to become a Hyndburn councillor for 30 years and a Mayor in 1988.

At this point, the sea crossing was very dangerous but Cliff's fear was overcome by the excitement of his first sea voyage aboard a Cunard vessel.

Having safely docked at the bottom of 50th Street, Marxist writer and photographer Robert

Cliff Westell today

Kappa joined the ship as they sailed onwards to Halifax in Canada and then the Arctic Circle. Cliff describes Kappa as the "finest war photographer" and the pair struck up a firm friendship.

"He was on board for three weeks and he really introduced me to politics and Marxism. There was a lot of spare time out at sea and we would discuss politics and really try and put the world to rights. Robert had a great impact on me and was a great man - a true inspiration. It was a tragedy when he was killed by a landmine in 1951.

"The year after, I was in New York again and was given a copy of an article Robert had written about that trip for the Saturday Evening Post. I even remember the first line of the story: 'We crept silently out of New York harbour....,' and with that very trip I made a good friend whose words I shall remember for as long as I live."

David Danger today

The soldier who cheated death...

"When people were being called up, I found out about a man who had a family so I volunteered to go in his place"

Words by Emma Mayoh

David Danger, aged 81, of Fulwood, Preston, was an SAS soldier who cheated death on a daily basis as he battled through forests in the Le Morven region of France as a wireless operator.

He parachuted into the area near Dijon on June 10 as part of A Squadron, 500 miles behind enemy lines and four days after sea craft landings on the beaches.

He was called up from a post in Egypt with the Royal Signals. He said: "I landed there in the top of a tree and had to cut myself down. The area is almost all dense forests and an ideal place for hiding in. But it meant of course that it was ideal for the Germans to hide in too.

"We were the first ones into that area and we had to make sure the other squadrons coming in after us made it down safely. There were squadrons from France and Belgium and the second SAS squadron that came in after us that I helped bring in. We parachuted in to stop the German forces getting through the Belfour Gap over the mountains towards Strasbourg where Hitler was sending in more troops to go and help those down at the D-Day battles. The squadron I was with was part of the early stages of the SAS led by Major David Stirling which disbanded when he was captured and when the war finished but was formed again three years later to make the SAS we know today.

"I saw a lot of horrible things and lost a lot of my friends. But it was important to carry on. I had to make sure that air supplies were guided in and that we rescued any pilots who had to evacuate their planes in an emergency. I was most at risk of German snipers who were ordered to kill radio operators first so our communication would be cut. When people were being called up, I found out about a man who had a family so I volunteered to go in his place.

"There were eight who came forward at first but once we found out what it would involve, just two of us decided to go. I've told all my experiences to an author who's writing a book about SAS soldiers and it's great that memories are going to be permanently captured in text.

"I was in the SAS for three years and it was always dangerous for me with the role I played. I've actually spent five years going back to the Le Morven region trying to find all the graves of my friends who died out there and I've finally managed to do it.

"It was important to me because we all looked after each other and made sure we kept our chins up even at the bleakest of times. We always made sure we worked as a team and did everything we could to avoid being captured. After that, I moved up into Norway and was there until the war ended."